Igniting the Heart

Kate Bruce has done congregations a great service by offering preachers a feast of ideas, insights and worked examples on the underexplored theme of preaching with the imagination. Her analysis is anchored in careful theology and attentive awareness of the contexts and cultures in which preaching is offered and received. The result is a gracious, well-argued and timely book, a treat-in-waiting for all preachers still alive to their task.

Bishop John Pritchard

Tired of dull boring sermons with no theological depth? And tired of dull boring books on preaching which equally lack theological depth? This book is the solution! Kate Bruce is an outstanding practitioner and teacher of preaching. Out of that expertise she shows how the interaction of the imagination with both the biblical text and contemporary culture can transform the preaching event and allow God to work in exciting and relevant ways. Honest, humane and humble, this is the book for all preachers who have a passion for God to speak.

Revd Professor David Wilkinson, Principal, St John's College Durham

Expect to be enriched, challenged, encouraged and inspired by this book. Kate Bruce argues that the sermon is essential in the life of the Church and that imagination is essential for preaching that ignites the heart. An exploration of the theology of imagination and language, examples from sermons, models of preaching and guidance for good practice are offered in a book that will appeal to a wide readership. I commend this book to all preachers who hope that through their sermons God will be encountered as the Spirit breathes life into their words and hearts are warmed.

Revd Ruth Gee, Chair of the Darlington District of the Methodist Church

Just occasionally weary preachers stub their toes against treasure hidden beneath the surface of a well-trodden path. In this book Kate Bruce draws on her considerable experience as school teacher, parish priest, theological college tutor and stand-up comic. With an assured grasp of homiletic theory and a passion for creative sermon construction, she shows us how the imagination can disclose new worlds, turn our assumptions upside down, provoke us to ask 'what if?' and help us live in the minds of other people. In this she follows the example of Jesus who did not despise the parable, the haunting image, or the disturbing paradox. This is a book for preachers who would prefer their sermons to dance and sing rather than trudge, hobble and plod.

David Day

Kate Bruce skips the conventional wisdom related to preaching and tackles the peculiar challenges and demands of the craft itself. She walks the reader through the creative process towards a fuller realization of the sacramental imagination. Her valuable book will remind us all – whether beginner or busy pastor – to love and cultivate the art we practice.

Richard Lischer, Duke Divinity School, author of *The End of Words and Reading the Parables*

Igniting the Heart

Preaching and Imagination

Kate Bruce

scm press

© Kate Bruce 2015

Published in 2015 by SCM Press
Editorial office
3rd Floor, Invicta House
108-114 Golden Lane,
London EC1Y 0TG.

SCM Press is an imprint of Hymns Ancient & Modern Ltd
(a registered charity)
13A Hellesdon Park Road
Norwich NR6 5DR, UK

www.scmpress.co.uk

British Library Cataloguing in Publication data

A catalogue record for this book is available
from the British Library

978 0 334 05319 4

Typeset by Manila Typesetting Company

Printed and bound by
CPI Group (UK) Ltd, Croydon

Contents

This book is dedicated to David Day on behalf of the many, many people who have benefited from his inspirational preaching and outstanding teaching of the art of preaching.

Acknowledgements

Huge thanks go to David Wilkinson and Jeff Astley, who supervised the PhD underlying this book. Thanks to them for wisdom, patience and insight.

Many thanks to Maeve Sherlock for time spent reading and commenting on a draft, and assuring me that she hadn't lost the will to live.

To the students who have been part of the preaching classes at Cranmer Hall over the years: thank you for your generosity and engagement. I hope I taught you at least as much as I learned from you.

To all the delegates at the Durham Preaching Conferences, as well as friends in the College of Preachers and people who have attended preaching events I have offered nationally: thank you for your support and encouragement.

This book would never have been written without the permission-giving congregations with whom I have worked; people who have joined me in the serious 'play' of preaching and given me space to try, to fail and to learn. Thank you especially to Holy Trinity Ripon, St John's College Durham, St Oswald's Durham and St Mary Magdalen, Belmont.

Thank you to colleagues at Cranmer Hall for your friendship and for covering my workload, enabling me to take a period of study leave to finish the PhD. Thanks too to colleagues in CODEC (www.dur.ac.uk/codec) for your challenge and imagination.

Much of the work behind this book was undertaken as Fellow in Preaching at CODEC. This post has been funded by contributions from Bible Society, Joseph Rank Trust, Halley Stewart Trust and the Maurice and Hilda Laing Trust. Thank you for your generosity.

Thanks also to the Women's Continuing Ministerial Education Trust Fund for contributing to the cost of PhD fees.

And finally, to all those rather fabulous people who have cheered me on over the years: thanks – you know who you are.

And finally, finally, underpinning it all, my deepest thanks to the Master Preacher.

Introduction

Picture the scene. It's Wednesday. You are sitting at the dining-room table surrounded by scribbled notes on screwed-up pieces of paper. You have done your homework. You read the passages earlier in the week and have been praying and pondering over them. You've now focused on and wrestled with the text, identified possibilities and difficulties, chased down ideas in commentaries, prayed and pondered some more and yet you have nothing concrete to work with. The laptop is fired up, but you are not.

Meanwhile the clock is ticking.

Sack it all. You snap the lead on the dog and head for the hills. The internal panic monster growls in your ear. As you walk, ideas and snippets of the text come to mind and drop away. A possibility starts tugging at your sleeve, but as you turn to look it flits off – a half-baked idea, it is dismissed. Returning home, other things press in and occupy your attention. The sermon worries are set aside. Meanwhile, as yet unnoticed, deep in your imagination something starts to stir.

At this stage in the sermon preparation process I have learned to trust that somehow it will come together – an approach that mugs the panic monster. When I return to focused preparation I discover that while my conscious mind was dealing with the day to day, the sermon was taking shape. Something seems to have happened in the incubator of my imagination. Impressions gathered as I strolled through the biblical landscape might tug insistently at my sleeve. Odd thoughts connect with ideas I might have picked up in a commentary or a conversation. Perhaps overheard snippets from the supermarket queue will float into consciousness and offer themselves as illustrative material. Scripture speaks to Scripture and sets up resonances. Links are forged: a scene from a film; a picture in the paper; a headline; a Facebook comment; a line from a song; a Tweet. Seemingly random materials seem to fuse together and the sparks start flying. The structural framework emerges from scribbled ideas. Scripture, image, day-to-day instances and applications are welded into shape; form and content inform each other.

I picture the preaching space and play with delivery ideas as I pace around the living room: gesture; eye movement; use of space; tonal variation; verbal emphasis. The dog looks quiz-zical. I rehearse possibilities on the stage of my imagination, playing with the sermon material, hammering it out on the anvil of possibility. I find myself engaged, absorbed and focused. The blue touch-paper is lit. The heart ignites. Boom. We are on our way.

This is invariably my experience in sermon preparation, which is a process that takes me through the valley of creative despair (where I have no ideas and on a bad day don't want the hassle), up to the heights of delight in the privilege of exploring with people the power of the ancient text alive in the present moment, inexorably pulling us towards the love of God.

Of course, working on a sermon prior to the delivery is only half the story. Arguably the sermon doesn't become such until it is delivered live in the event. Here the lifeless text or notes become the sermon as the preacher interacts with the congre-gation, and in that specific context the Spirit breathes life into dead words. Some ideas are dropped; improvisation might lead to new thoughts and ideas as the preacher works on their feet, responding to the nudge of the Spirit in the moment of delivery. As they speak, the sermon leaves them and wings its way to the hearer, where it might take a new shape as it fuses with themes in the life of the whole community; in this person's current life experience; in that person's present concerns or hopes. As different hearers apply aspects of the preached material to their own situation, other sermons are heard, birthed from the one preached.

Perhaps this view of preaching is too positive. It is also true that the sermon may die in stony cynicism, become buried in the soil of distraction or *worst of all* nosedive into the barren rocks of boredom. The day of the poorly conceived, ill-prepared, dull, disconnected, boring, irrelevant, authoritarian, yawn-inducing, patronizing, pontificating, pointless and badly delivered sermon is *most emphatically over*. However, I want to go in to bat for the enduring power of the sermon. Imaginatively conceived and delivered, guided by the revelatory impulse of God, the sermon has the potential to move and inspire people; in short, it can ignite the heart.

The image behind the title for this book, *Igniting the Heart*, suggests a sense of words pulsing with revelatory potential, leaping out and sparking connections in the imagination of the hearer. This is an understanding of preaching laden with illuminating possibility, the 'Aha' moment when the switch flips, the lights go on and we see anew. For preaching to ignite the heart, it must spark connections with the hearer. Achieving such connection requires the active engagement of the imagination of the preacher and hearer.

The imagination is of vital importance for preaching. In all the stages of the sermon process the human imagination, filled with the revelatory power of God, is at work: in prayer; in biblical spadework; in observation and reflection; in mulling and contemplation; in the unconscious fusion of ideas; in the play of words on the page; in the forging of empathetic connection and the logical linking of ideas; in the work of performance; in the task of reception and action. Imagination matters to preaching.

This book explores how we might helpfully understand the work of imagination and why it matters so much to preaching. It examines the theological and practical consequences of this and offers preachers ways of strengthening their imaginative muscle. With this in mind, imagination needs to feature in homiletics teaching, both as a subject in its own right and as a factor shaping the approach to the structure and delivery of curriculum content. The purpose of this book is to inspire and equip preachers and homiletics teachers to be imaginative in the way they think about, prepare and deliver sermons.

A word on terminology: the discipline of homiletics is here understood as the theoretical and theological underpinning of the practice of preaching. Preaching is defined as the design, delivery and reception of an oral event, which is based, in some form, on Scripture and earthed in a particular cultural context. It rests on the theological principle that God is a God who communicates, who speaks in many ways, the sermon being one such place of divine encounter, and one with a long and worthy pedigree in the life of the Church. Preaching occurs usually – though not necessarily – in a liturgical setting, involving hearer as well as speaker. It is created in the hope that hearts will ignite and individuals and communities find themselves challenged and changed.

The lie of the land

Arguing for the vital importance of imagination for the preacher, we need to be clear about what the imagination does. Chapter 1 explores various understandings of imagination and offers a framework designed to help us map aspects of the function of imagination.

Mindful that connecting imagination with preaching might create anxieties about linking the sermon to that which might be dismissed as fantasy and illusion, Chapter 2 offers a theology of imagination to demonstrate the central importance of imagination in the life of faith. This will serve to guard against the worry that in linking preaching and imagination the truth claims of the gospel are in any sense negated. On the contrary, the contention is that imagination and revelation are inherently linked. The aim is to demonstrate that imagination is a vital tool of theology and essential to effective preaching.

Chapter 3 explores imagination and language, offering a model of preaching that is open to learning from the work of the poet. It is part of the function of imagination to paint with language designed to be evocative, appealing, daring and invitational. This chapter explores this theme, arguing for lyrical preaching as opposed to the more prosaic, flattened language of 'settled reality' and 'pervasive reductionism'.[1] This is preaching as poetic speech that seeks to peel back the layers of inanity and tedium and disclose new hope, new vision and new possibility. Lyrical preaching is marked by a desire to grasp imaginatively the disclosure of the gospel and to render that seeing and its implications by learning from the craft of poetic expression. Imaginative preachers, alive to the disclosive potential of words, will give thought to shaping the language they are using, deliberately writing for the ear.

Linked to this, Chapter 4 argues that preaching has sacramental potential, the divinely graced imagination of preacher and hearer enabling a fresh disclosure of God. The sermon can enable the 'Aha, now I get it' moment when our eyes are opened to a deeper apprehension of reality. This is the insight that occurs when the curtains are drawn back and we catch a glimpse – albeit 'through a glass darkly' – of the Infinite Other. There are voices today calling for the end of the monologue sermon, on the basis that preaching is authoritarian, top-down speech that renders the hearer as little more than a receptacle.[2] Preaching at its worst can become this. However, at its best it is laden with revelatory potential, which means it should not be abandoned; instead preachers need to ensure that what they deliver is authoritative rather than authoritarian, supportive rather than oppressive, seeking to meet the hearer as a co-pilgrim along the way.

---

1 Walter Brueggemann, *Finally Comes the Poet: Daring Speech for Proclamation*, Minneapolis, MN: Fortress Press, 1989, pp. 4, 6.

2 David C. Norrington, *To Preach or Not to Preach: The Church's Urgent Question*, Carlisle: Paternoster Press, 1996; Doug Pagitt, *Preaching Re-imagined: The Role of the Sermon in Communities of Faith*, Grand Rapids, MI: Zondervan, 2005.

Imagination is vital in preaching, not only in terms of informing how we shape and express content and recognizing its sacramental richness but also in how preachers imagine their role in the preaching event. How preachers see themselves directly affects how and why they engage in the task. Preachers' master metaphors matter since they carry theological freight that will have practical outworking. Chapter 5 explores potential master metaphors for the preacher – preacher as teacher, herald, artist, spiritual director, jazz musician and jester – and makes clear how these might affect theological understandings of the purpose and praxis of preaching.

The final chapter concludes with the question every good preacher has near at hand: 'And so what?' The implications are pulled together to conclude that imagination is vital to preaching; that imaginative muscle can be strengthened and must be developed as a spiritual discipline. The preacher needs to engage with imagination at each stage of the sermonic process and be willing to develop new approaches and performance methods. Allied to this, the vital place of imagination in preaching will affect the way homiletics is taught.

I

Imagination –
What it is and Why it Matters

'Imagination' is a slippery word and difficult to pin down. How can we speak of it with any precision? Ask yourself a simple question: 'If I were to try and describe "imagination" to an alien, what would I say?' Asking the question of a group of preachers always generates a variety of responses. For example:

- Seeing something as something else.
- The opportunity to dream with all your senses on red alert.
- Creating new ideas about a product or task.
- Thinking of things in their absence.
- Thought about what *could* be.
- Playful cognitive escapism.
- Pictures behind the eyes.
- Seeing beyond the normal limitations.
- Imagination – thought unbounded.
- Seeing new connections between things.
- Dreaming of possibilities.
- Daydreaming.
- Putting yourself in someone else's shoes.
- Creating in the mind experiences we've never had.
- Recalling the past.
- Seeing from another point of view.
- Playing with mental Lego.
- The ability to act a part.
- Seeing what could be instead of what is.
- Bringing life to a different reality from the one present.

- Exploring the question, 'If this, then what?'
- Creating the idea of an alternative reality.[1]

This range of response, not untypical of ideas generated by other groups, associates imagination with a wide range of functions: forming mental imagery; recollection; empathy; forging new connections; supposition and hypothesizing; intuition; seeing one thing in terms of another; thought; creativity; playfulness; shaping vision; dreaming; fantasy and escapism. Given the range of responses here, can we be confident about what we mean by imagination?

Framing imaginative function

As we can see, people come to the question of imagination with many different ideas. When homiletics tutors urge students to be imaginative in their preaching, what exactly are they asking for? Are they advocating the use of poetic images and illustrations to enhance the clarity of the rational points, placing imagination in the position of handmaiden to reason? Are they urging the use of a narrative style to embody the whole meaning conveyed in the sermon? Maybe they are suggesting innovation in form, structure and performance. Perhaps they want preachers to inhabit the scriptural text from the perspective of a particular character. Or are they commending an empathetic evaluation of the hearers' context? Are they advocating the use of supposition and 'If this, than what?' thought experiments, feeding a prophetic edge to the sermon? Maybe they want to provoke their students to ask how they imagine themselves in the preaching role and reflect on how that affects their approach to the task. This range of possibility suggests that confidence in the clarity of the term 'imagination' is misplaced.

---

1 Ideas crowd-sourced from students and staff at Cranmer Hall, St John's College, Durham.

Given the complex variety of understandings of imagination, homiletics could benefit from a framework of imagination, enabling us to conceive clearly of the range of imaginative function, allowing for coterminous expression and collaboration between its various expressions. Mary Warnock offers the following description of imagination, which usefully pulls together many of the areas referred to above:

> There is a power in the human mind which is at work in our everyday perception of the world, and is also at work in our thoughts about what is absent; which enables us to see the world, whether present or absent as significant, and also to present this vision to others, for them to share or reject. And this power . . . is not only intellectual. Its impetus comes from the emotions as much as from the reason, from the heart as much as from the head.[2]

Four areas of imaginative function emerge from this: the way we see things in everyday perception; how we make connections and present that 'seeing' to others; our emotional experience; our intellectual processes. We can affirm and enhance Warnock's understanding of imagination by describing it under four headings:

1 The sensory function.
2 The intuitive function.
3 The affective function.
4 The intellectual function.

The sensory function

Some might shy away from talk of the imagination on the basis that it is the skill of the artistic few. However, Warnock reminds us that it has a vital role in 'our everyday perception

---

2 Mary Warnock, *Imagination*, London: Faber & Faber, 1976, p. 196.

of the world'. In the sensory function, the imagination draws from sensory data and enables the formation of images in the mind. Without the image-making potential of imagination, sensory information would overload us – we would not be able to process incoming data through similarity and categorization. Although our experience of the world consists of fleeting impressions, the sensory function of imagination enables us to conceive of continuity, identifying and labelling similarity and difference, perceiving of objects being in absence and recognizing ourselves as beings in time. This provides a sense of continuity to our existence. Without this sense of being persons with a past, present and future, our identity would fragment – we would have no sense of individual selfhood or of belonging to communities with histories, existing in the present with responsibility for the future. The sensory function is essential to our well-being.

It is useful to see the sensory function contributing to the work of imagination in its reproductive and productive modes. In reproductive mode, the imagination reproduces from accumulated sensory data what our perception cannot directly access. Even though perception occurs from a standpoint and we never see all of what we are looking at, our seeing is not partial but holistic – imagination supplies what we cannot see, filling in the gaps in perceptual view.

With the imagination operating in its more productive mode, we can play with the materials of sense perception to create something we couldn't perceive in objective experience. Drawing from the data banks of material gathered in by the senses, combining, separating and recombining, we can explore different realities, possibilities and outcomes. There is an argument here for preachers to engage with the scriptural text and contemporary context with the senses on high alert, drawing in materials that can be creatively reworked and connected in the formation of the sermon.

Ignatius of Loyola encourages an imaginative approach to the biblical text that draws on the sensory and can be an important step in noticing details that might otherwise have been missed, especially with familiar passages. It is worthwhile to try to read the ancient text of the Bible with the sensory imagination fully engaged. What would it mean to walk the landscape of this world? What would we see, taste, touch smell and hear? The imaginative preacher ventures on a field trip into the pages of the Bible, foraging for sensory details and throwing them into the knapsack for later consideration. In such imaginative engagement the two-dimensional printed word stands up and wraps the reader in its horizons. This method works particularly well with vivid narrative text. Readers place themselves in the scene, watching it unfold on the cinema screen of imagination, being sure to discipline the output of imaginative engagement by the actual detail of the text. If the ancient text lives for the preacher, they can paint it in words for the hearer to step in and ponder. Such Ignatian exercises reveal where we stand in the text and can contribute to our exegesis and self-understanding.

One of the tasks of the preacher is to take the written word of the scriptural text and animate it in the preaching moment, the printed word becoming three-dimensional, enlivened, filling the space and drawing us in. The following extract from a sermon on the Raising of Lazarus demonstrates the power of the sensory imaginative function to make a scene pulse with life. Read it aloud and identify how the preacher makes the scene vivid. How do they draw on the sensory imagination and seek to feed the sensory imagination of the hearer?

Let's jump right into the climactic moment of John 11
The crowd gather around Lazarus' tomb, jostling and jockeying for pole position.
Hear the mixed murmurings of compassion, anxiety and disapproval.
The babble of the bewildered.
Jesus frowns, greatly disturbed.
At his command, and in spite of Martha's horrified objection about the stench of death, they heave the stone aside.

Some recoil, aghast.
Some crane forward, intrigued.
Horror and hope displayed on the faces.
Jesus' voice cuts through the air.
He prays, calling on God, 'that [the crowd] may believe that
you sent me'.
Silence.
[Hold pause]
Then the cry:
'Lazarus, come out . . .'
Some strain forward into the open mouth of the tomb.
What do they see?
Shuffling awkwardly, 'The dead man came out, his hands and
feet bound with strips of cloth, and his face wrapped in a
cloth.'
What do you see?[3]

It's clear the preacher has walked the landscape of this story
with sensory imagination on high alert. Use of strong verbs
creates a sense of dynamic movement, capturing the high drama
of the narrative. The preacher is alive to the soundscape of
the scene, the babble of the crowd in response to these strange
events. Note too that the sense of smell, however distasteful,
is not overlooked. Reasonably, the preacher pauses, holding a
silence in the preaching moment that reflects the likely silence
and shock in the gathered crowd as the stone is rolled back
from the tomb. The silence is broken by the cry 'Lazarus, come
out'. This causes some in the crowd to 'strain' forward, creating
a sense of tension and anticipation. In terms of what they see,
the biblical text is quoted directly: 'The dead man came out, his
hands and feet bound with strips of cloth, and his face wrapped
in a cloth' (John 11.44). Shifting the question to the congregation, 'What do you see?' invites hearers to imagine themselves

---

3 The full text of this sermon is found in the Appendix.

in the scene, as onlookers. In just a few lines a preacher alive to the sensory imagination can create a powerful retelling of the biblical narrative, drawing hearers into the scene.

At the heart of good exegesis is close observation. As well as exegeting the biblical text, preachers need to observe their preaching context closely, exegeting the signs and symbols of the communities in which they preach. The imaginative preacher needs to be a keen observer of life, a 'snapper up of unconsidered trifles',[4] filing away observations from Scripture, nature, news, relationships, popular culture and literature. Preachers on high sensory alert can gather a wealth of impressions to help them exegete context and congregation.

Are there architectural features that inform understanding of the history and values of these hearers? What do the noticeboards tell us, or the news-sheets? How does the church represent itself in the wider community? Is there a magazine? Is there any digital presence, and what story does it tell? Listening to the stories the community tells itself is a useful way of reading the context. What events are happening in this church? What seems to matter most? What hymnody is chosen? What theology is being framed in the music? Does the building smell fresh and clean or fusty and old? Is it cared for or neglected? Preachers on high sensory alert can gather a wealth of impressions that can be used to shape and inform their understanding of the context, which will have some effect on the content, shape and delivery of the sermon. Referencing aspects of the building in the sermon itself can help to earth it, hooking it into the fabric of the building. While this attention to detail is not always possible for visiting preachers, it is a useful strategy for preachers embedded in their context.

Our ability to draw on sensory data to create scenarios that do not presently exist is crucial in preaching. At a particular point in time a community might be facing crisis, with no obvious perceivable resolution. The imagination is not bound by the limits of this situation, but free to take wing and create

---

4 Shakespeare, *The Winter's Tale*, Act 4, scene 3.

a different 'reality'. This is not to be dismissed as building 'castles in the air'. Arguably, where there is no power to change the present situation, the imagined possibilities of a new reality in themselves can bring the power to endure and to hope, allowing longing to be expressed. The point is that we can never become what we cannot imagine, so a community in bondage will always be so until someone finds the imaginative power to declare that they 'have a dream' and to sketch out their dream to others. Part of the task of preaching is to bring to words an alternative vista of possibility through an act of the sensory function reading the current context, drawing on memory and allowing the intuitive function to envisage new possibilities. Imaginative power can lift our eyes beyond the immediate to focus on the transcendent, setting the immediate in the context of the eternal – always the bedrock of Christian hope.

The intuitive function

Picture a pan on a low heat. Hear the pan lid knocking as the contents simmer, the flavours blending and the temperature rising. What's cooking? The intuitive function is at work. This cannot be hurried. No rushing too fast to an end point. No allowing the ticking clock to force the process. A good sermon cannot be written in one sitting; there needs to be space and time. So the ingredients are left on the back burner. The pot will come to the boil in time. If we try and rush too quickly from ideas to finished script, the result is always undercooked, half-baked and indigestible.

In its intuitive function, imagination expresses itself in flexibility, in making connections and seeing beyond the obvious, conventional and literal. Intuitive imagination sees patterns and makes links; it transposes, reorders and rearranges material. In this sense, intuitive imagination has a vital function in forming figurative language, minting metaphors and employing poetic insight and craft. It can raise possibilities by combining material to forge new and surprising images, enabling a new 'seeing'. Interestingly, much of the work of the intuitive function takes place beyond our consciousness. Many preachers will attest to reaching a point in preparation when they find themselves surrounded by scribbled notes and stumped for a way forward. Perhaps after going for a walk, or sleeping on it, the insight comes in a sudden rush, as if from nowhere. The spark comes and the fire burns. Given this, there is wisdom in ensuring that sermon preparation allows time for the blending and fusing work of the intuitive function – or valuable insights may be lost.

In intuition the imagination takes us beyond seeing in the sense of sensory perception and embraces 'seeing-as', or 'aspect perception'. Ludwig Wittgenstein demonstrated this in Jastrow's famous duck–rabbit figure.[5] We see exactly the same drawing and yet in a moment of insight we suddenly interpret the data differently and something new emerges – either a duck or a rabbit.

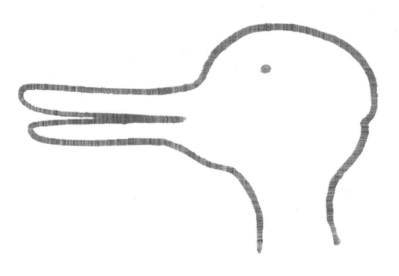

5 Ludwig Wittgenstein, *Philosophical Investigations*, trans. G. E. M. Anscombe, London: Blackwell, 1968, pp. 194–5.

In the duck–rabbit example the shift in seeing is sudden – one moment we see the duck, then suddenly the rabbit. Exactly the same data is interpreted in a new light; something new emerges in a sudden rush. A similar event to the duck–rabbit shift in seeing can happen as we consider a scriptural text. We see it one way and then something new emerges from the familiar landscape of the text.

In a concept similar to 'seeing-as', Donald Evans writes of 'on-looks'. An 'on-look' implies greater commitment than an outlook or perspective.[6] On-looks are a way of describing how we look on the world and our part in it, and they help to shape our character, as well as our relationships. Part of the preacher's task is to name, encourage or challenge our on-looks. What are our typical on-looks of God, other and self? How do we look upon the poor, weak and despised? What is our on-look of the Church: body of Christ or social club? Naming and framing the right questions is an intuitive, imaginative act, which requires noticing and naming attitude and behaviour that are often habitual and therefore overlooked. In this sense the sermon acts as a mirror in which we might see ourselves reflected back.

Sometimes the connections made by intuition are quirky and unusual as the imagination engages with material in serious playfulness, enabling us to 'see a world in a grain of sand, /And a heaven in a wild flower'.[7] Preaching is an artistic, theological event that seeks to encourage and enable on-looks that inspire new ways of living.

Given that the intuitive function helps us to see beyond the obvious, it has a role in shaping sacramental seeing. How does a person apprehend anything of the divine in the ordinary or of the majesty of God transcendent? We can only do this through the grace-filled engagement of the imagination in its

---

6 Donald Evans, *The Logic of Self-Involvement*, London: SCM Press, 1963, p. 125.

7 William Blake, 'Auguries of Innocence', www.artofeurope.com/blake/bla3.htm.

intuitive function, which can lift our vision to a perception, albeit 'through a glass, darkly' (1 Cor. 13.12 KJV), of divinity. In this sense faith must always call upon acts of intuitive imagination, using the material gathered from the world of sense perception to create figurative forms, pictures that pull back the curtains, enabling us to catch a glimpse of transcendent reality.

The intuitive imagination makes connections, challenges on-looks and fuses the horizons of the biblical text and the contemporary context, shaping figurative language to help engender new insights. Examine the following extract from a sermon on John the Baptist, based on Matthew 3.1–12. How does the preacher demonstrate the intuitive imagination at work?

On the brink of the season of excess,
John the Baptist's voice
cuts through the growing aroma
of mulled wine and mince pies.
Never mind the Iceland and M&S ads –
John gives us
winnowing forks and unquenchable fire.
Penitence. Judgement.
Provocative themes.
Challenging. Troubling. Scary.
John.

Last in the line of the Old Testament Prophets –
an edgy Elijah figure:
no rich fabrics,
no fine cuisine.
What kind of royalty does he herald
in his camel-hair robe?
This uncompromising locust-cruncher,
this wilderness wanderer.
His message insistent, uncompromising –
Baptizer John – bringer of heartburn.

> Heart. Burn –
> the searing awareness
> of compromise and failure;
> it's John who strikes the match.
> Can you feel your heart strangely warmed?
> *Repent. Reconsider. Reorientate,*
> *'for the kingdom of heaven has come near'!*[8]

The extract above sets John the Baptist's on-look against the usual on-look inhabited by many of us in the run-up to Christmas. In the clamour of consumerism and excess, the penitential season of Advent is often lost. In an attempt to recapture this, the preacher fuses the horizon of text and context, bringing John the Baptist's message cutting into the present moment. The familiar world of Iceland and M&S adverts, mulled wine and mince pies, is juxtaposed with John's winnowing fork and unquenchable fire. Continuing to highlight the sharp judgement in John's message, the preacher plays on the double meaning of heartburn: the implicit result of seasonal excess elides with the sense of the heart burning with guilt. Language relating to fire, a symbol of judgement, is woven into the piece: 'unquenchable fire', 'heartburn', 'searing', 'it's John who strikes the match'. The question, 'Can you feel your heart strangely warmed?' deliberately alludes to Wesley's conversion and introduces a note of comfort alongside the harshness of John's message. Not all hearers would make this connection, but it is planted there for the knowing to pick up, and those who miss it will not lose the main drive of the sermon. The extract displays a seriously playful approach to language, a quirky connection between ideas and a desire to uncover and challenge our seasonal on-looks with the on-look of John the Baptist.

---

8 The full text of this sermon can be found in the Appendix.

The affective function

Both sympathy and empathy are aspects of the affective imaginative function that are important for preaching. We can regard sympathy and empathy as operating on a continuum, with sympathy as 'near-by' affect and empathy as 'inside' affect. The latter requires a much closer imaginative identification with the situation of the other. Empathy is epitomized in the advice of the lawyer Atticus Finch to his daughter in Harper Lee's novel, *To Kill a Mockingbird*: 'You never really understand a person until you consider things from his point of view . . . until you climb into his skin and walk around in it.'[9] It requires that the one trying to understand the feelings of the other imaginatively projects themselves into the other's situation. Empathy opens up the potential for vicarious experience, which carries with it the possibility of increased knowledge and understanding. We engage the affective imagination when we feel for characters in a novel or film, when we consider their situation as if we were in it ourselves. When we read the news and project ourselves into the situation of the other, the affective imagination is at work. Arguably, the affective imagination is the driver for our intercessions. Engaging empathetic imagination can generate deep compassion for those who are very different from us, generating the possibility for new insight. Richard Eslinger regards empathy as essential in preaching as it enables us to 'live into a context not our own',[10] which can transform our attitudes and understanding.

The affective imagination can make present what is absent in terms of the perspective and emotions of another. For example, the preacher at a funeral – assuming they have no connection with the deceased – is likely to have a sympathetic approach to the mourners but not necessarily an empathetic connection. In sympathy, grief is witnessed from more of a distance. They

9 Harper Lee, *To Kill a Mockingbird*, London: Heinemann, 1960, p. 35.
10 Richard L. Eslinger, *Narrative and Imagination: Preaching the Worlds That Shape Us*, Minneapolis, MN: Fortress Press, 1995, p. 102.

preacher can *choose* to adopt a more empathetic stance towards the mourners by engaging imagination. In order to preach in a way that connects with the potential range of narratives in the room, the preacher can consider the various potential affective states, such as grief, shock, anger, guilt and relief. In these empathetic imaginings, the preacher needs to draw from their own more distant grief experiences, to avoid the danger of shifting into too close an empathetic identification, which will hamper their ability to manage the funeral effectively.

In all preaching preparation the affective imagination is profoundly important for the preacher's reflection on text and context. In terms of textual exploration, Ignatian prayer techniques draw heavily on the skills of the affective imagination. Central to Ignatian spirituality is the view that imagination has revelatory potential. In imaginatively considering the experiences of the characters, new insights can be experienced. In affective imaginative engagement with the text, sympathy can move into empathy as we shift from imagining – for example, Peter's desolation following his denial, as if we were Peter in the biblical narrative – to feeling our own guilt and shame connected with the stories of our own denials of Christ. Similarly, with the Parable of the Prodigal Son we can sympathetically imagine the joy of the younger son, welcomed home in celebration, or we can draw closer and empathetically feel with him the Father's welcoming embrace. In this understanding there is more affective distance with sympathy than with empathy: sympathy is 'near-by' affect; empathy is 'inside' affect.

David Heywood points to congregational lack of interest as being a key barrier to listening, compounded by sermons that are too difficult to understand. He recommends listening to the passage 'with the ears of the congregation'.[11] He is implicitly pointing to the importance of exercising the affective function of the imagination. The imaginative preacher considers the hearer's perspective, asking questions such as: What questions

---

11 David Heywood, *Transforming Preaching: The Sermon as a Channel for God's Word*, London: SPCK, 2013, pp. 36–7.

is this passage likely to spark? What are the objections it might generate? How might people feel about this idea or that illustration? If preaching is to ignite the heart, it must appeal to people's affective capacities, and this is an inherently imaginative undertaking.

If preaching is to stimulate and handle affect responsibly and appropriately, then preachers need to be aware of the power and potential, as well as the associated dangers, of using strong affective approaches. Affect needs balancing with reason, logic and reflection. People should never leave a sermon feeling they have been emotionally manipulated or exploited. Wise and healthy affective engagement can build up the sense of continuity between the individual, their community and wider contexts. Such imaginative function is the antidote to a fragmented, myopic individualism that stunts vision, damages identity and community and destroys the impetus to engage in a life founded on the ethic of neighbour love.

The following is an extract from an Easter Day sermon based on John's account of the resurrection (John 20). How does the preacher use the affective imagination and seek to engage the affective imaginations of the hearers?

It's difficult for many of us, but try and imagine you had never heard John's account of the resurrection before.
'Early on the first day of the week, while it was still dark . . .'
The clues are all there.
The first day of the week.
The first day of something new: at this stage neither Mary, nor the uninitiated hearer, realizes just how transformative, cataclysmic and wonderful that something new will be.
'While it was still dark, Mary Magdalene came to the tomb.'
'While it was still dark' – the language points us towards the gloom of Mary's grief and lack of understanding.
Let's try and home in on her point of view:
She has witnessed the horrific death of a man to whom she was devoted.

She was there at the foot of the cross.
She was there when the spear was jabbed into his side.
She was there when the blood and water poured out.
She was there as his mother and the other women wept.
I imagine she watched as the body was taken down, wrapped in cloths and sealed up in the garden tomb.
What did she feel as the stone was rolled into place?
Can you imagine?
Have you heard the sound of earth falling on a coffin lid?
If you have, really heard it, then you have some insight into Mary's darkness.
It is a terrible darkness.
It is the darkness that snuffs out hope,
a suffocating creeping darkness that erodes any belief in a future.
It is the poisonous, insinuating darkness of death.
It's bleak.
And yet . . .
And yet . . .
There is a competition going on in the first line of this passage.
'Early on the first day of the week, while it was still dark . . .'
Darkness dominates, yes, but we know that dawn is coming – a thought worth clinging to in those times when we wrestle with depression, illness, grief and struggle.
Yes – darkness might surround us now –
but with God, dawn from on high will break upon us.
It always comes, following even the wildest, blackest nights.
Yes – the night hours are long, but nothing can stop daybreak.
Here in John 20 verse 1 we have the Christian hope encapsulated in the image of the early morning darkness.
The darkness must fade.[12]

---

12 The full text of this sermon can be found in the Appendix.

The opening move is to try to put the hearer into the position of not knowing the outcome of the story, implicitly asking them to stand in Mary's shoes. The theme of darkness as Mary experiences it is explored, with reference to her gloom and grief and lack of understanding. The flashback to things she has witnessed strengthens the vicarious experience of inhabiting her perspective. The preacher makes the assumption that Mary witnessed the deposition and burial of the body. This is a faithful handling of the text since John tells us she was present at the cross, and she knew where the body had been laid. Trying to get the hearer to begin to connect with the enormity of Mary's grief, the preacher uses a very strong example, connecting the emotion generated by the sound of the tombstone being rolled into place to the sound of earth hitting a coffin lid. There is such finality in that sound. Anyone who has heard it will come much closer to understanding Mary's position. The danger with such a strong image is that it will take people into their own memories of grief and that this will overshadow the turn to hope in the sermon. However, a softer example would fail to capture the deep sense of Mary's loss. If resurrection is to be preached effectively then death needs to be named honestly. The turn to hope is signalled by a return to the first verse, 'Early in the morning on the first day of the week, while it was still dark', picking up on the dark/light motif in the passage and expanding the field of reference to incorporate darkness, depression, illness and struggle. This means that the dawning of resurrection hope embraces all human suffering, a move that shows the preacher seeking to stand affectively with those in difficulty and point to the dawning of light. In this sense the sermon paints an alternative vista of possibility informed by trust and hope in the resurrection.

The intellectual function

Recognizing the intellectual function of imagination helps us to avoid polarizing reason and imagination and enables us to see that imagination is not simply about fantasy and feeling. Imagination is not bracketed off in a category separate from rational thought. Rather it is a resource that reason can employ. Hypothesizing, a reasoned step-by-step process, constructed around an 'if . . . then' model of supposition, involves the imagination in a projection of what might happen and what could be possible. This skill of hypothesizing is an inherent aspect of the intellectual imagination.

The writer, preacher and poet George MacDonald passionately advocated understanding the role of imagination in science, claiming, in 1893, that the 'prudent question' comes from the imagination, which suggests new directions in research and enables the 'scaffolding of hypothesis' without which 'the house of science would never rise'.[13] Only 23 years prior to this, when the physicist John Tyndall delivered his 'Discourse on the Scientific Use of the Imagination' to the British Association for the Advancement of Science, the response from *The Times* was scathing, polarizing imagination against the skill and patience of observation and experiment.[14] Such polarizing of imagination and intellect is misconceived, and the importance of imagination in science is now widely accepted.

For example, Thomas Kuhn[15] described the scientific process as research based upon a paradigm – a body of widely accepted knowledge that shapes how we look at the world. This involves the spadework of research, exploration and experimentation. In Kuhn's analysis, as research progresses anomalies will occur that do not fit the accepted paradigm. While these may be resisted for a time, eventually they lead to a crisis point followed by a sudden, revolutionary shift into a new paradigm. The shift in seeing that Kuhn describes comes as a result of effort, learning,

---

13 George MacDonald, 'The Imagination: Its Function and its Culture' (1867), www.gutenberg.org/files/9393/9393-h/9393-h.htm.

14 Lorraine Daston, 'Fear and Loathing of the Imagination in Science', *Daedalus* 127:1, Science in Culture (Winter 1998), pp. 73–95.

15 Thomas Kuhn, *The Structure of Scientific Revolutions*, 3rd edn, Chicago: University of Chicago Press, 1996.

trial and error and the application of hypothesis and supposition. Here the intellectual function of the imagination is at work, which may contribute to a sudden realization and a new seeing. An important aspect of the intellectual imagination is the willingness to notice anomalies and to risk and question the 'irrefutable' evidence of the old paradigm. The intellectual imagination involves a willingness to follow such observation and search beyond the accepted status quo.

Some sermons, drawing on the logical skills of the intellectual imagination, will employ reason, supposition and hypothesis, marshalling thoughts to present an argument, anticipating and countering objection in the quest to persuade the hearer. They may employ aspects of other imaginative functions but the driving force is the logic of reasoned discourse arguing for a new perspective. The movement of conversion is itself a paradigm shift, as an old version of reality is set aside and a new one embraced. While conversion might be seen as a matter of affect, it is also a movement of 'if . . . then' logic.

One of the interesting aspects of supposition is that we can engage in it without having a commitment to its truth content. We can invite a congregation, in which some may be highly sceptical, to suppose in imagination that the resurrection – for example – occurred and imaginatively explore the possibilities of that supposition, even if their current experience is to doubt or deny such a possibility. In such suppositional engagement lies the invitation to faith, which is essentially rooted in the question '*What if* the gospel accounts of the nature of God are true?' 'Were they to be true, *then what?*' This is fundamentally an imaginative question with the potential to affect our perception of reality. This argument assumes that there is a connection between our imaginative explorations and the potential effect they have on our apprehension of the external world. What goes on in imagination affects who we are and how we live. One of the tasks of homiletics is to encourage suppositional questioning in the fields of faith and ethics with the aim of opening up the potential for transformation. In short, this means stimulating the intellectual function of imagination.

The following is the text of a sermon preached in the context of a university carol service. In what ways is the preacher seeking to engage the intellectual imagination of the hearers? Try to identify the key stages in the argument. Where and how does the preacher anticipate and address potential congregational objection?

I'd like to begin with a quotation from that profoundly inspirational book by Dr Seuss, *How the Grinch Stole Christmas*:

And the Grinch, with his Grinch-feet ice cold in the snow, stood puzzling and puzzling, how could it be so? It came without ribbons. It came without tags. It came without packages, boxes or bags. And he puzzled and puzzled 'till his puzzler was sore. Then the Grinch thought of something he hadn't before. What if Christmas, he thought, doesn't come from a store? What if Christmas, perhaps, means a little bit more?[16]

I wonder what might Christmas mean to you?
Tinsel and trimmings?
Turkey and Twiglets?
The ritual glass of sherry left out with a carrot?
Family fun?
Family feuds?
Romance and mistletoe?
Not having enough money?
The tyranny of the Christmas-card list?
Carols and candlelight?
The wonder of the midnight service?
Christmas comes to us wrapped up in experiences and expectations: happy times, difficult times, traditions and tunes.

---

16 Dr Seuss, *How the Grinch Stole Christmas*, Random House, 1988.

John Betjeman, one-time poet laureate, in his poem 'Christmas', explores the question of what Christmas is: he wanders through the symbols and sights of Christmas, before finally arriving at a crucial question:

> And is it true? and is it true?
> The most tremendous tale of all,
> Seen in a stained-glass window's hue,
> A Baby in an ox's stall?
> The Maker of the stars and sea
> Become a Child on earth for me?[17]

Let's peel back the layers and with John Betjeman and the Grinch – a delightfully unlikely pairing – ask the question, 'What if Christmas, perhaps, means a little bit more?' 'And is it true? and is it true?' Did it really all happen?

Did God, Creator of all, really take on human flesh?

Was God really born, a baby who became a child, a boy, a man? Did God really become flesh and walk among us?

Embrace the leper, feed the hungry, party with the undesirables? Annoy the religiously correct?

Did they really hang him up to die on a wooden cross on a rubbish tip – mocked and despised?

Did they really bury him in a tomb and seal his body up?

Three days later did he really meet with Mary in the garden in the early light of day?

Did he really rise again?

Did he really promise his followers that he would always be with us?

If the answer to those 'did he reallys' is a 'yes', then Christmas means an eternity more than our tinsel and trappings might suggest. If it's true, we can't separate Christmas, the account of Jesus' birth, from the accounts of his life, death and

---

17 John Betjeman, 'Christmas', *Collected Poems*, London: John Murray, 2006.

resurrection. And if it's true we can't separate that great story of God with us from the stories of our lives. It's all of a piece and it changes absolutely everything.

That is, of course, if the answer to those 'did he reallys' is 'yes'. If the answer is 'no, none of it is true', then we can shrink-wrap Christmas, reduce it to tinsel and trimmings, turkey and Twiglets, call it the Holiday Season, knock back a Christmas cocktail. End of story.

But this question 'Is it true?' is not so easily dismissed. It's like a burr that sticks. Is it true?

The Bible attests to it.

Countless people through the centuries have experienced the truth of the gospel transforming their lives.

Countless people have demonstrated the truth of the gospel in the effect they have had on the world.

Ask Martin Luther King – 'Is it true?' and listen to his preaching and look at its effect.

Ask Corrie ten Boom, 'Is it true?' and speak to the Jews she hid from the Nazi SS.

Ask Archbishop Desmond Tutu, 'Is it true?' and observe his courage in speaking out against apartheid.

Ask countless ordinary people 'Is this true?' and hear stories of lives remarkably changed.

And yet we resist. We throw up questions like roadblocks:

What's the status of the Bible anyway?

Why is there suffering if God is so good?

Why is there such evil in the world?

Good questions – but often used not in a quest for an answer but as a way of avoiding the underlying question. Is it true? Is it true?

We throw up barriers. Yes – there are lots of great people whose lives attest to the truth of the gospel. Famous people and little-known folk.

But then we line up against that list the religious attitudes that are thoughtless and small-minded; Christians who have annoyed and insulted us, those stereotypical killjoys. Thus we construct a defence that stops us even starting to explore the question of truth.

Most people aren't atheists; most people just dismiss the question, put it aside, embracing agnosticism in the heart of the party season. I know. It was my strategy. 'Anyone who actually believes in Jesus – well, come on . . . Mostly quite nice people, but all clearly insane. God might exist, who knows, but I mean, it's mad. Isn't it? Jesus and all that. It's all vaguely embarrassing.'

So for me the question of truth was shoved aside.

But that burr wouldn't go away.

Always the underlying nag: but what if it is true?

Why did people bother to record the birth, life, death and resurrection of Jesus in the Scriptures?

Why do people give their lives for it?

How is it that this belief prevails?

How is it that people who are intelligent and wise and not generally given to insane statements, point to this faith and say in their actions and their words: 'This is true'?

So I began my tentative journey inching out into the world of faith; testing, questioning, anxious not to be conned, but unable to resist the question, 'Is it true?'

A few years back I met a woman called Gill

She was coping with a terminal illness, which for her rather sharpened the question of truth.

We explored the idea of faith being like that invisible bridge in the Indiana Jones film. Gill explored the possibility of God as she approached her death. Inch by inch, question by question, prayer by prayer she began to walk across that invisible bridge of faith. Step by step she discovered through her experience that God is to be trusted – the bridge can more than bear the weight. As she walked a very dark path, she discovered the light of Jesus shining brightly in her times of fear and pain.

Gill risked dismantling her internal roadblocks of resistance to the possibility that it's all true.

So what did she do in her exploration? She crept into church and sat at the back, listening. She began to talk to God and to listen to God. She picked up a Bible and began to read it and ponder. She began to articulate for herself the possibility 'What if . . .?'

What if it is all true?

What if it isn't all futile?

What if there is an ultimate power that created the universe?

What if that ultimate power came into the world?

What if that ultimate power was born to a poor couple on a particular night at a specific juncture in history, with a particular name: Jesus?

What if that Jesus came into the world for a specific purpose?

What if Jesus came to free us

from the tendency to snatch resources to ourselves;

from the dead-end corridors of our narrow-mindedness;

from our foot-stamping will to power;

from our lust to have and hold what is not ours;

from the tangible darkness of our deepest fears;

from the swamps of yesterday's shame?

What if Jesus came to set our feet on a rock, to invite us along a new way –

the way of forgiveness and love, through death into his life?

In which case – Christmas means a little more than turkey and Twiglets.

As I wrote this, I was aware that in a strange sense I was writing it for just one person. I don't know your name, I don't know what you look like. You are a silhouette centre stage in my imagination. You are drawn to the question, 'Is it true?' Part of you longs for it to be so. But part of you dreads it. You worry that if you begin to explore this question of truth, you will be hemmed in by other people's expectations; trapped into a closed religious system of do's and don'ts. Worse still, your friends might think you are a fool.

But so often we are already locked into systems of expectation: Academic expectations – hard work and first-class marks.

Social expectation – be popular and have lots of friends, and in due course marry and have a family.

Economic expectation – get a good job, car, house, holidays in the sun and so on.

God is not calling us into yet another closed system of expectation but on to a journey of faith, forgiveness, love, new possibility. There are plenty of varieties of fool in the world. Happy the fool who is in pursuit of something that matters.

So for all of us this Christmas, can we hear the whisper of God:

'Yes. It is true.

Yes. You are included.

Yes. My love is for you.

Yes. Follow me and become who you are truly called to be.'

Can we answer God's 'yes' to us with our 'yes' to God?

The quiet whisper of the human heart to the heart of God.

Perhaps we are inching out on to the bridge of faith, early steps; or perhaps we are far out across the span. Each of us is invited to trust that God will lead us to the next step. As simple as that.

> And the Grinch, with his Grinch-feet ice cold in the snow, stood puzzling and puzzling, how could it be so? It came without ribbons. It came without tags. It came without packages, boxes or bags. And he puzzled and puzzled 'till his puzzler was sore. Then the Grinch thought of something he hadn't before. What if Christmas, he thought, doesn't come from a store? What if Christmas, perhaps, means a little bit more?

The key question of the meaning of Christmas is raised through the playful device of the extract from *The Grinch Who Stole Christmas*, using this as a springboard from which to ask the hearer what Christmas means to them. Often lines from songs or references to films or books can be used to anchor a question or reflection, earthing the spiritual in the material. A variety of examples are layered that open up possibilities regarding the meaning of Christmas. The extract from the Betjeman poem enables questions of meaning and truth to be raised through a delightfully unlikely pairing, marrying 'high' and 'low' culture. The layering of 'Did God/they really?' questions enables a swift summary from incarnation to resurrection and the promise of the Spirit. The drive of the argument is that if the answer to the posed questions is 'yes' then that changes everything. If the answer is 'no' then Christmas is simply a seasonal holiday. However, the question of truth is not easily dismissed. The evidence of the biblical witness and human witness is cited, before objections are raised as the preacher seeks to anticipate congregational objection. The argument is that our objections, while often being excellent questions in themselves, tend to be used as roadblocks that stop us even getting to the exploration of the question of truth.

The preacher then draws from their own story of faith development and the key factors that led to their continued exploration: both the fact of the biblical witness and the examples of people who pointed to the truth of the story. The example of Gill is offered, with the image of faith as a journey over a bridge. The layering of 'What if?' questions allows the call to freedom to be set against the human condition, leading to the conclusion that if the Christmas narrative is true, it changes everything.

The focus on the imagined listener is a device that allows the preacher to name the longing and dread likely to be present at least in some of the hearers – longing for truth but fearing expectations. The point is raised that we are all to a degree caught up in expectations but God's invitation is into a journey of hope and possibility, not a closed system of expectation. This leads into the gentle suggestion of response, with the image of inching out across the bridge of faith. The Grinch quotation bookends the sermon, allowing the question 'What if Christmas, perhaps means a little bit more?' to be raised again.

Key questions to establish in sermon construction

There is a logical step-by-step argument underpinning this sermon. The preacher is seeking to take the hearer on a journey that raises questions and explores possibilities. There are four key questions to which the preacher needs to be alert:

Who am I addressing?

Identifying your audience is crucial. At a carol service there are a whole range of people gathered. The sermon above was aimed at the sceptical university student attending out of tradition and loyalty to the college community. At the same time the piece also sought to offer encouragement to the faithful and a reminder to keep looking beyond the seasonal trimmings.

What do I want to convey?

The example wrestled with the question, 'Is it true?', identifying the 'it' as the birth, life, death, resurrection and ongoing presence of Christ, seeking to convey the importance of this question and the weight of the answer. The overall message was of God reaching out to the hearer, with an invitation into the journey of faith.

How do I want to convey my message?

Given a potentially closed and sceptical hearer, the tone here was playful, honest and gentle. In naming their own scepticism and struggle, the preacher sought identification with the hearer, offering themselves as a fellow pilgrim walking alongside.

How do I want my hearer to respond?

The hope was that the hearer would give the question of truth some consideration – be willing to move out further on to the bridge of faith. The underpinning theological understanding was that for many people, conversion is a journey into faith, owing more to the model of the road to Emmaus (faith dawning gradually) than the Damascus road event (faith coming in a sudden rush).

The intellectual imagination helps in structuring a logical reasoned argument, which calls for seeing the flow of the discourse, identifying cracks in the argument and taking remedial action. Cicero saw the art of public speechmaking as teaching, delighting and persuading. Persuasion means helping someone to see the anomalies in their current position and move to a new apprehension.

Taking someone on that journey calls for an imaginative awareness of where they are and of how they might be moved. Logic, hypothesis and supposition, aspects of the art of persuasion, belong in the toolbox of the intellectual imagination.

The framework of imaginative function

The framework helps us to speak about the variety of ways the imagination operates. To summarize: the sensory function of imagination draws from the material of sensory experience to bring images to mind; the intuitive function works with the material of sense perception to make leaps and connections, helping us to see things in new ways; the affective function is linked to the imaginative ability to empathize and see from another perspective; the intellectual function is associated with the imaginative capacity for reason, hypothesis and supposition. Imagination, in all its functions, is vital to preaching. The following chapter demonstrates the central importance of imagination in the work of theology and the task of preaching.

2

A Theology of Imagination

Imagination is vital to all our theology, and preaching is one expression of the theology of the Church. As such it should be profoundly imaginative. However, associating imagination with preaching may raise a theological offside card. Doesn't this association open up preaching to the accusation that it's all mere fantasy? What are the theological foundations for the assertion of the importance of imagination?

A clear sense of imaginative function indicates that fantasy is only one aspect of imagination, and also that fantasy, in the shape of storytelling, can be a vehicle of truth and discovery. The theological foundations for the assertion of the importance of imagination lie in the content and form of Scripture, as well as some key theological concepts: revelation, incarnation, the divine character and the *imago Dei*. Linked to this, a theology of play, an inherently imaginative undertaking, will be developed and applied to preaching. With the caveat that there are limits to the power of the imagination, the aim here is to show the centrality of imagination in the theological task and hence in the event of preaching.

Imagination and Scripture: problem, mandate and use

Scripture: a problematic picture?

On first consideration, the biblical material relating to imagination is problematic. There is no single word used in the Bible correlating to the English term 'imagination', though there are a number of words, in Hebrew and in Greek, that carry connotations of the term.[1] *Yatsar*, meaning 'to form', is used of God's creation of humans and animals (Gen. 2.7, 8,19), and the majority of its 62 occurrences relate to divine creative activity. *Yatsar* can also mean 'purpose' or 'inclination', as in 'every inclination of the thoughts of their hearts was only evil continually' (Gen. 6.5). Similar usage is found in Genesis 8.21, in which God resolves never again to destroy the earth even though the 'inclination of the human heart is evil from youth'. In its 52 occurrences, the Hebrew word *machăshăbăh* conveys meanings ranging from the devising of works of art and decoration for the Temple (Exod. 31.4; 35.32, 33, 35), to the thoughts, devices and plans of the human heart (e.g. 1 Chron. 28.9; 29.18; Job 5.12; Prov. 12.5). *Maśkiyth* occurs six times, and its meanings vary from a carved figure or an idol (Lev. 26.1), to a picture (Num. 33.52) or an imaginative conceit (Prov. 18.11). Much more common is the word *lêb*, occurring 589 times and meaning the inner self, heart, mind, will, resolution and seat of emotion, source of courage, conscience and understanding.

In the New Testament there are a number of terms that bear some connotations of our understanding of imagination. *Meletao*, meaning to devise or contrive, occurs three times: 'When they bring you to trial and hand you over, do not *worry beforehand* about what you are to say' (Mark 13.11). 'Why did the Gentiles rage, and the peoples *imagine* vain things?' (Acts 4.25). '*Put these things into practice*' (here the KJV reads '*meditate upon*', 1 Tim. 4.15). These three usages all relate to a sense of inner reasoning, cogitation and projection. Closely linked to this, occurring 14 times, is *dialogismos* – conveying a sense of inner reasoning, thought or deliberation, as well as doubt,

---

1 Alison Searle, '*The Eyes of Your Heart': Literary and Theological Trajectories of Imagining Biblically*, Milton Keynes: Paternoster Press, 2008, p. 32.

disputation and argument.[2] The word *dianoia*, occurring 13 times, relates to the mind, to understanding, desiring and feeling. It occurs in the commandment to love God with heart, soul and *mind*. In Ephesians 1.18 it is translated variously as 'the eyes of your' 'understanding' or 'heart'.[3] Finally there is the term *kardia*, occurring 160 times, meaning the heart, the centre of physical and spiritual life and the source of passions and desires; it is the inner world of the person, the source of good and bad contrivance.

The biblical concept of the heart conveyed by the words *lêb* and *kardia* offers a good basis for a theology of imagination. The heart is the spiritual, intellectual, moral and ethical centre. As Proverbs counsels, 'Keep your heart with all vigilance, for from it flow the springs of life' (Prov. 4.23). According to the Psalmist, 'Fools say in their hearts, "There is no God." They are corrupt, they do abominable deeds; there is no one who does good' (Ps. 14.1). In Genesis the wickedness of humanity is located in the 'inclination of the thoughts of their hearts' (Gen. 6.5). Similarly the beatitudes understand purity of heart as having a connection with seeing God, in the sense of recognizing, apprehending and understanding, with the correlate implicit meaning of living out that purity in practical ways. The heart is associated with decision-making, being the source of David's decision to build a house for the Lord (1 Kings 8.17). The heart is also portrayed as a centre of emotion, the spring of joyful worship and gladness, as well as grief. In Romans, Paul pictures the heart as the centre of belief. Oral expressions of faith need to be supported by deep-seated heart-belief:

> if you confess with your lips that Jesus is Lord and *believe in your heart* that God raised him from the dead, you will be saved. For *one believes with the heart* and so is justified,

---

2 See Matt. 15.19; Mark 7.21; Luke 2.35; 5.22; 6.8; 9.46; 9.47; 24.38; Rom. 1.21; 14.11; 1 Cor. 3.20; Phil. 2.14; 1 Tim. 2.8; James 2.4.

3 See also Mark 12.30; Luke 1.51; 10.27; Eph. 2.3; 4.18; Col. 1.21; Heb. 8.10; 10.16; 1 Peter 1.13; 2 Peter 3.1; 1 John 5.20.

and one confesses with the mouth and so is saved. (Rom.
10.9–10)

Overall, the biblical picture of the heart is that it is in need of
change. The prophet Ezekiel expresses the divine promise: 'A
new heart I will give you, and a new spirit I will put within
you; and I will remove from your body the heart of stone and
give you a heart of flesh' (Ezek. 36.26). The imagery of a stone
heart conveys the sense of deadness and coldness in the biblical
view of the heart without God, and underscores the centrality
of the heart in steering thought, determination and action. The
correlation of the biblical idea of the heart with the concept of
imagination is illuminating for the preacher. What is the purpose of preaching if not to enable a new apprehension of God,
life, the other and the self? This is a call to reimagine, to see
anew and orientate the will around that new vision.

Biblical form: a mandate from Koheleth

As important as biblical content is for grasping a sense of
the scriptural view of imagination, the form and style of the
sacred texts is also significant. The picture painted of Koheleth,
the eponymous author of the book of Ecclesiastes, seeking
out proverbs and setting them in particular order, while also
searching to 'find just the right words' (Eccles. 12.9–10 NIV),
conveys in microcosm the biblical focus on the importance of
form. The wide-ranging genre and the powerful use of poetic
imagery convey a sense of the role of the imagination in shaping
and communicating biblical ideas. The corollary to this is that
engaging with the Bible calls for active imagination in interpret
ation and application. To read the text as though meaning can
be extracted and the form cast aside like mere wrapping is to
fail to see the imaginative connection between what is said and
how it is conveyed. The content and form of the Scriptures convey to the preacher a sense of the need to engage imaginatively
in the creation of sermonic content and form.

In examining the commonplace elements in the content of the parables alongside the artistry of their construction, we see the imagination encompassing the everyday aspects of perception as well as more artistic creativity. The imagination is at work in the parables, particularly in its sensory and intuitive functions (see Chapter 1). The imagery of the parables is commonplace – coins, bread, neighbours, sheep, fields, vineyards, fish, nets and so forth. Jesus takes the sensory data of his everyday context and, in a fusion of intuitive insight, gives new twists to familiar stories. In his use of figurative language, Jesus communicates a call to think creatively about the use of story, anecdote, resonant image and subverted expectation. The parables invite reflection on how to engage people's imagination, using structures that imprint on the memory in order to challenge, confront and comfort the hearers.

Preaching after the pattern of Jesus' imaginative example means to particularize the abstract in the concrete, using the currency of resonant, contextual images that will speak the astonishing universal into the specific, the ordinary and the mundane. Earthing the abstract idea is a task of the imagination in all its functions. Using the sensory function, what does the preacher notice in the ordinary that can be drawn upon to give an example or instance – a slice of life to make the abstract concrete? Employing the intuitive function, how might images, ideas and stories be fused in arresting and unusual ways? Drawing from the affective function, what emotional responses might this material both communicate and generate? Exercising the intellectual function, how does this image or idea feed into the overall logic of the sermon structure? What objections might be raised and how could they be countered?

Analysis of Nathan's parable of the lamb in 2 Samuel 12 is instructive in the discussion of imagination and preaching, as it is a good example of the use of graspable image and story that combine to create a highly effective piece of communication. The parable follows David's adulterous liaison with Bathsheba and his subsequent successful murder plot. The prophet uses

33

a secular story to effect change, underscoring the power of fiction to draw people to God.

> and the LORD sent Nathan to David. He came to him, and said to him, 'There were two men in a certain city, one rich and the other poor. The rich man had very many flocks and herds; but the poor man had nothing but one little ewe lamb, which he had bought. He brought it up, and it grew up with him and with his children; it used to eat of his meagre fare, and drink from his cup, and lie in his bosom, and it was like a daughter to him. Now there came a traveller to the rich man, and he was loath to take one of his own flock or herd to prepare for the wayfarer who had come to him, but he took the poor man's lamb, and prepared that for the guest who had come to him.' Then David's anger was greatly kindled against the man. He said to Nathan, 'As the LORD lives, the man who has done this deserves to die; he shall restore the lamb fourfold, because he did this thing, and because he had no pity.' Nathan said to David, 'You are the man!' (2 Sam. 12. 1–7 NRSV)

The features of the parable are drawn from a world with which the primary hearer, David, is familiar. Structurally, the piece is woven around the narrative staple of the rich man and the poor man. The form and content are tightly woven with an incremental use of pathos; the layering up of words and images designed to provoke an emotional response. The rich man with his '*very many* flocks and herds' is contrasted with the poor man who had '*nothing but one little ewe lamb*'. The parable shows how the choice of a single word can increase a particular effect; note how less effective the word 'sheep' instead of 'lamb' would have been. The pathos builds with reference to the lamb being brought up with the poor man's children and sharing his '*meagre fare*'. This lamb, from being brought up with the man's children, nursed as a child, becomes like a daughter to him. Before the tension can break into the release of laughter, the subject is abruptly changed through the device of the traveller, who is structurally important in terms of carrying the shift of focus but also useful in that he presents familiar content in terms of the need to provide hospitality. The meanness of the rich man is emphasized as we recall that with his '*very many* flocks' he has ample resources from which to provide for the needs of his guest. The narrative trap is sprung as the wealthy man helps himself to the poor man's lamb and David erupts in a rage that will shift to penitence as he recognizes himself in the rich man's actions.

In this parable we see clearly how an imaginative approach has the power to confront and challenge and be heard. Nathan comes at David's sin obliquely and appeals to his imagination. The story gets under the wire of David's defences and disarms him. Had Nathan simply denounced David's behaviour out of hand, would he have been able to lead him into repentance? Nathan is operating out of a 'hermeneutic of spiritual direction',[4] helping to restore David's relationship with God by enabling him to see his behaviour clearly and recognize his sin.

The process of imaginative recognition seen in David's response to Nathan's story is important to scriptural engagement in general and preaching in particular. As we make connections with perspectives and characters within the Scriptures, we are drawn closer in, invited to recognize our own voices in the cadences of the lament psalms, our own weaknesses in Peter's denial or Judas' betrayal, or our own potential in the humanity of Christ. In such imaginative recognition we encounter something of the divine shaping effect of Scripture.

Imagination as theology's vital tool

Might we actually suppose imagination itself to be a vital tool and resource for our grasp and elucidation of the substance

---

4 Kay L. Northcutt, *Kindling Desire for God: Preaching as Spiritual Direction*, Minneapolis, MN: Fortress Press, 2009, p. 7.

of theology, enabling us, in certain circumstances at least, to go further and to see more than other more discursive modes of theological reflection?[5]

There are a number of reasons why this proposal might be resisted. Linked to fantasy, idolatry, deceit, delusion and evil, imagination might not appear too congenial to the theologian. However, imagination can be defended on the grounds that, like any other aspect of humanity, it can be employed to positive or negative ends. Temptation may come in the shape of images and inner narratives, but resistance can also be mediated by the same means. That imagination can be abused is no reason to oust it from the theological arena. Imagination can be seen to operate in Christianity in four ways: narrative, in the stories of faith needing absorption and visualization; metaphorical, in the handling of the figurative language of Scripture; visionary, in the insight of the seer; and as a cognitive mode in theology.[6] These modes are all relevant to the task of preaching. How do we retell the stories of faith effectively, bringing them off the page with colour, movement and texture? This is a task of the imagination, as is the handling and framing of figurative language to enable the spark of new insight. It is the exercise of imagination that brings the preacher down from the cloudy world of concepts, earthing abstraction in the concrete.

The imagination helps us to see patterns, learning to recognize and name God's interaction with us. This is not always straightforward in the midst of difficult times. However, as we look back we can often discern the divine fingerprint that helps us to reframe our experience and see it against the backdrop of God's presence with us. Identifying God's presence, even in hindsight, gives us hope in the present moment with God and frees us from limiting self-definitions, enabling us to anticipate

---

5 Trevor Hart, 'Imagining Evangelical Theology', in *Evangelical Futures: A Conversation on Evangelical Method*, ed. John G. Stackhouse Jr, Grand Rapids, MI: Baker Books, 2000, p. 192.

6 Eva Brann, *The World of the Imagination*, Savage, MD: Rowman & Littlefield, 1991, pp. 705–6.

and live into a future redeemed from the sin we commit and the evil that befalls us.

Imagination: the human point of contact

Imagination can be seen as the anthropological point of contact between revelation and human experience.[7] Imagination is the locus of revelation not because of any inherent connection it has with God but simply because it is the point in our experience where revelation is encountered.

> It is the imaginative power – the God-given way humans are hardwired – that provides the locus for transcendent revelatory truth to be revealed.[8]

The content of revelation is an act of grace but it is received by an ordinary, human capacity – that of imagination. Imagination can be linked to fantasy and deceit but the point remains that it is also related to truth and discovery. There are things that are real but cannot be directly apprehended physically. In terms of the subatomic level, or in the field of cosmology, physical realities are present but we cannot spatially apprehend them. The natural sciences and theology both make use of paradigms, models that draw from the everyday world, in order to enable the 'seeing' of realities that transcend the ordinary.[9] Similarly God is real, objectively present but not apprehended directly. An aspect of preaching is to draw from the everyday to open our eyes to the cosmic reality of God and the imagination is inherently important in enabling such seeing.

Figurative language plays a key role in divine revelation, which comes to us in ways that mostly, though not exclusively,

---

7 Garrett Green, *Imagining God: Theology and the Religious Imagination*, Grand Rapids, MI: Eerdmans, 1989, p. 29.

8 Sandra M. Levy, *Imagination and the Journey of Faith*, Cambridge: Eerdmans, 2008, p. 103.

9 Green, *Imagining God*, pp. 61–80.

appeal to imagination. Scripture pulses with imagery designed to open our eyes to a deeper and richer apprehension of the nature of God. Such imagery lodges in memory and shapes faith: 'The Lord is my shepherd'; 'behold I stand at the door and knock'; 'the lion will lie down with the lamb'. Linguistic images add incrementally to our understanding and help us to see more profoundly than we do when we pursue the illusion of trying to nail God down with fixed, precise description. The importance of figurative language in the Bible, as bearer of revelatory potential, strengthens the argument that preachers need imaginative sensitivity in handling such tensive structures and skill in creating them. This is explored in further detail in Chapter 3.

Imagination and interpretation

There is a sense in some interpretive approaches to the Bible that the text lies static in the distant past and we must mine for its proper meaning. In many ways this seems a reductionist view of revelation. It is useful to imagine scriptural authority in the Church in terms of a moving stream rather than a changeless deposit.[10] In this analysis, imagination builds on the tradition, bringing together an attempt to discover the original focus of the author, the way the text has been interpreted in various stages during the past, and the current context.[11] If we are to avoid arid bibliolatry and embrace an understanding of the lively, present, local revelation of God, this picture is worth consideration. As the preacher connects the present moment with the biblical text, we see Scripture breathing anew in a different context. If we see revelation as fixed and finished, the task of the preacher is to extract the meaning from the text and teach it. This leads to an account of preaching that is

---

10 David Brown, *Tradition and Imagination: Revelation and Change*, Oxford: Oxford University Press, 1999, p. 127.

11 Brown, *Tradition and Imagination*, p. 55.

overly rational, takes no account of genre, nor the context of the preacher's life, nor the situation of the hearers.

Preachers nervous of the implications of this might find some assurances in controls that judge our imaginative construal of God's revelation. The tradition exerts a controlling effect on the preacher's imaginative construal. 'Tradition' embraces the nexus of creedal confessions, liturgical forms and Scripture, grounded in the decisive, historic occurrence of the life, death and resurrection of Christ and earthed in the context of the faith community. Often the 'faith of the Church' seems to mean the opinions and ideas of the official theologians of the Church, ignoring the *consensus fidelium*; that is, the views of the body of the faithful, past and present, which has a role in determining revelatory truth and is an important guard against arrogance and prejudice.[12] Here 'ordinary theology'[13] is absolutely essential for the preacher. Ordinary theology is the content and articulation of the theology of Christians who have not received scholarly education but whose theology is earthed in practice. The congregation should be recognized as a control on the imaginative formulations of pulpit talk. They are part of the preaching event, they bring their experiences of faith lived out in daily life and they are the body of Christ. At the very least, preachers should listen to the theology of their hearers and ensure that there is space for them to question and explore sermonic content. This could be through a simple device such as a table for sermon discussion during coffee after the service or, better still, preaching preparation groups that draw on the faith and experience of the community in shaping the sermon.

Moral criteria also help to weigh the assertion of revelatory impulses present in an imaginative construal of a text in a particular context. For example, reflection over time in western

---

12 David Brown, *Discipleship and Imagination: Christian Tradition and Truth*, Oxford: Oxford University Press, 2000, pp. 404–5.

13 Jeff Astley, *Ordinary Theology: Looking, Listening and Learning in Theology*, Aldershot: Ashgate, 2002.

culture has led away from a view that women and children are chattel, and any attempt to demean their humanity in the name of God would fall foul of this moral control. Indeed, unreflective propositional preaching on Pauline passages that suggest that women should be silenced or subject to oppressive headship teaching also falls foul of this control.

The role of the Spirit, 'God's imagination let loose',[14] is helpful at this juncture. The radical nature of sin disrupts and endangers human apprehension of the presence of God. Self-interest, entrenched views, stubbornness and stupidity can blind us to discerning God's revelation among us. The Spirit poured into human hearts enables right seeing. The Spirit acts as guide and prompt in the process of sanctification. In such activity we see God reaching out in love into the situation of sinners, shaping, guiding and creating new possibilities.

The imaginative work of God's Spirit activates imaginative response in the recipients in terms of cognition and creativity. In cognitive terms the Spirit enables us to apprehend the world through a new paradigm in which the world is eternally related to God, and it is God's story that shapes, holds and judges all other stories. This is not to dismiss all other stories, in a narrow outlook that brooks no alternatives, but rather to live out of this paradigm with the conviction that this is the truest way to view existence. The Spirit captivates the imagination in all its various functions. This can be seen as part of the expression of God's imagination working in us and through us to engage with others.

Incarnation: a divine act of breathtaking imagination

In the incarnation the immanence of God is magnified in a way that had not occurred before; it creates a human history for God. This presents a new way of revealing the nature of God

---

14 John McIntyre, *Faith, Theology and Imagination*, Edinburgh: Handsel Press, 1987, p. 64.

and of God's interaction with humanity. This divine act of breathtaking imagination creates new stories; human imaginative reflections on God's central imaginative act. These Gospel stories tell of God with a face and fingertips, God with emotions, God who speaks in human tones and tells stories in familiar idiom. They become central stories in a new movement of God's Spirit in the formation and ongoing life of the Church. This is an act of daring, prodigious imagination.

Sometimes we are dull to this, blunted to the wonder by overfamiliarity. One of the greatest difficulties for Christians – preachers particularly – as the Christmas season approaches, is the question of how to capture a sense of the extraordinary imagination at work in the incarnation. We have heard the story, studied the doctrine, sung the narrative, absorbed it and assimilated it such that we have normalized it. Here a reduced imagination, numbed by seasonal spin, limits our vision. Seasonal sermons can easily boil down to 'Baby Jesus was born. Let's all be nice to each other.' The imaginative preacher will seek to come afresh to the ancient stories, seeking to subvert the seasonal saccharine, unwrapping the human longing for something more than turkey and Twiglets.

In Christ's story we find the answer to the human ache for something more. Here we find God in messy contact with the world. The God-man who understands hunger and sweat, longing and tears; Jesus who belly-laughs and mixes with undesirables; Christ whose perfect love reveals the shadows of hatred and hostility. When the darkness thickens around him, his beauty is seen in humility as he kneels to wash the feet of a denier and a betrayer and the feet of those who will flee. This flesh-God knows the fragility of the human form, beaten up and pinned to a piece of wood. He journeys ahead of us into the valley of death's shadow, and in the dawning light of the third day the old certainties are shattered. Death is overturned and new vistas of glorious possibility open up. Without this appreciation enlivening and underpinning our lives, our preaching becomes flat and joyless, pointless pontificating that crushes the soul. Preaching needs imaginative vision to see in Christ the beauty and perfection of God. This catches us up in the life-giving out-breath of divine love, filling heart and head and enabling new seeing, forgiveness, restoration and hope. Such 'seeing' sparks our delighted bewilderment in the sheer mystery, glory, love and presence of God. This awareness brings with it the invitation into the drama of relationship with God.

Drama in general has rich disclosive potential and as such is effective as a metaphor for our attempts to live out the gospel. It has many helpful entailments: the nature of God's character and how that is 'played out' in the incarnation; the shaping of our own character; our interactions with others in the parts we play; the scripts we work with; how we improvise in our playing of the gospel; what constitutes an authentic and 'faithful performance'.[15]

It is also instructive for the preacher to consider the discontinuities between drama and life. Most dramatic performance works with a relatively set script; the actor knows what is coming next in the plot and how they are supposed to react; they generally have plenty of rehearsal time. In contrast, 'the performance of life is more like a certain sort of improvised drama than the playing of a carefully scripted role'.[16] The Christian improvises around a script comprising cultural heritage, biblical material, theological learning and life experience; a script that is both similar to and different from those of other pilgrims. Our expectations and hopes are often thwarted by events, and we must work out how our script is performed and changed in the context of tragedy or unexpected joy. Finally, when the curtain closes on the final act down at the Hippodrome, the actors have a reasonable expectation of what comes next. When the curtain closes on our drama, it is imaginative hope that leads us to trust in another act.

---

15 Trevor A. Hart, 'Art, Performance and the Practice of Christian Faith', in *Faithful Performances: Enacting Christian Tradition*, ed. Trevor A. Hart and Stephen R. Guthrie, Aldershot: Ashgate, 2007, pp. 1–9.

16 Trevor A. Hart, 'The Sense of an Ending: Finitude and the Authentic Performance of Life', in *Faithful Performances: Enacting Christian Tradition*, ed. Trevor A. Hart and Stephen R. Guthrie, Aldershot: Ashgate, 2007, p. 175.

Preaching can offer a mirror to our life performance, helping us to interpret the biblical script and shape our own script in the light of this, as well as ideas for interacting with the more difficult characters we encounter. It can give us the permission to lament when devastation comes and to trust God in the midst of bewilderment, suffering and death. It can help us to shape our performance around that of Christ, trusting in the next act, alluded to in the garden in the early morning light. This eschatological hope will affect the way we perform, giving us a basis to look ahead with hope. If it lacks this imaginative vision, preaching soon becomes desiccated and pointless: the withered fruit of a stunted imagination, alienated from God, saying little and going nowhere.

Imagination: an aspect of the divine nature

Divine imagination is wider and wilder than we could ever dream of, and it is closer and more loving than we dare hope. God's imagination is at work in every aspect of creation from the heart of the cosmos to the heart of the tiniest insect and in the very core of our own being.[17]

Is it justifiable to conclude that creation expresses God's vast imaginative qualities? There are key reasons why this conclusion seems justifiable and necessary. From the rhinoceros to the millipede, notwithstanding the limits of natural theology, it is difficult to look at creation and not capture a sense of the imaginative scope of divine creativity. Even when people do not have categories of faith with which to frame their response to natural beauty, there is often a sense of peace, calm, awe or of the numinous sense of sacramental significance speaking through the natural world. The breathtaking beauty of creation inspires imaginative responses, as though we sought

---

17 Donal O'Leary, 'Imagination: The Forgotten Dimension', *The Furrow* 57:10 (2006), p. 525.

to echo something of divine creativity in human expression. We need to recapture a theology that sees God involved in nature in order to counter the economically driven approach to the earth's resources. Such a theology would seek to preserve and protect creation because it is in itself an expression of the beauty of God. In damaging it we damage ourselves as we destroy the beauty around us to feed the idols of wealth and comfort. Undoubtedly, creation bodies forth many signs of the divine imagination at work.

In the incarnation God inhabits the sensory world, drawing from his experience of the everyday to shape intuitive stories. In the mission of God seeking the lost sinner, exemplifying compassion and an understanding of the situation of the other, we see the divine imagination at work. In the risky work of redemption and sanctification we see the empathetic exercise of love, a dimension of the affective imaginative function. In Christ's teaching we see intuitive and intellectual imaginative power at work. Imagination is clearly an aspect of the divine nature.

Imagination: divine gift

In what sense can we see imagination as part of the *imago Dei* given to us as an essential part of our humanity, reflecting the divine imagination? The reference in Genesis 1.26–27 to humanity made in the image (*selem*) and likeness (*demut*) of God has been interpreted in a variety of ways. If we take the divine image as being associated with our capacity for *relationship with God*, *exercising dominion* and *reproduction*, we can start to build an argument that being created in the *imago Dei*, in the sense of any of these interpretations, implies the gift of imagination – a gift surely to be exercised in our speaking and reflecting on divinity.

Relationship with God requires imagination. Imagination can be seen as a devotional principle,[18] having a role in self-examination,

---

18 McIntyre, *Faith, Theology and Imagination*, pp. 84–7.

the reading of the biblical stories, the use of the Psalms – in which we place ourselves alongside the Psalmist, allowing their praise and lament, faith and hope to move us in prayer and worship – and in linguistic and visual imaging in prayer. We use imagination in seeking the will of God in the Scriptures as we imaginatively fuse the horizon of the biblical text and the situations of our own contexts. In relationship with God we know the reality of forgiveness and have some insight to help us to exercise forgiveness, an act clearly associated with the imagination. To forgive requires some sense of the reasoning of the offender, of their situation and motives; it calls for an act of affective imagining. One of the main tensions in the field of ethical praxis, often seen in struggles with forgiveness and in the area of spiritual development, lies between knowing the right course of action and not being able to act upon it. At the heart of many spiritual practices – such as spiritual direction, Ignatian prayer, journalling or meditative art – lies the work of the imagination enabling us to reach greater self-understanding and openness with the self, others and God, naming weakness and failure and being willing to envisage a different future. Confession is itself an act of ethical imagining, drawing on remembered failure and setting that next to the anticipation of life lived differently. It is a form of storytelling – 'This is the reality of my/our failure, but in the grace of God the plot-line will change.' Imaginative openness to the possibilities of God working with us in the present moment is an antidote to the cynicism that closes down, silences and separates people. The preacher can only preach effectively out of relationship with God, a relationship that calls on the exercise of imaginative faith in the day to day, flowing into the task of preaching.

Called to love God, we are also called to love neighbour as self. Imagination is key to the exercise of such love. An imaginative approach to the other will consider their present situation and the factors contributing to it, constructing from the parts of their history a sense of the whole and weighing actions carefully, anticipating the possible outcomes of certain words or behaviours upon the other while cultivating interaction that will bring about positive outcomes. An imaginative perceptivity exercised towards the other will engage with the story of how they arrived at a particular state. This may mean that the lover has a greater understanding of the predicament of the beloved than they have themselves, as when Jesus weeps over the sins of Jerusalem. Such imaginative engagement is more than simply a flood of feeling; it connects with the cognitive state of the other, seeks to appreciate the variety of pressures being played out and looks to take practical remedial action. This sensitivity to the other is a mark of the affective imagination at work. The human ability to love in such a way can be seen as a hallmark of being made in God's image.

This exercise of imaginative, affective love will shape the preacher's approach to the other, helping them to speak with empathy and compassion into the human condition. This builds congregational trust and reduces the likelihood of sermons full of thoughtless declamatory certitude of the 'should' and 'ought' variety – the equivalent of being beaten up with words. Affectively imaginative sermons show the preacher sitting with the objector, those who have failed, the faithless and the foolish and articulating the questions many are frightened to ask. 'Is it really true?' 'What difference does it make?' 'What if I can't forgive?' 'Why is it so hard to love?' 'Is God really there?' 'Why do such terrible things happen in the world?' Raising such difficult questions and responding honestly, with careful attention to Scripture, pointing people back to God's faithfulness, builds people up, develops trust and encourages community.

For all this the human imagination is vulnerable, often acting from either honest or masked self-interest. The fallen nature of humanity means that human imagination is flawed, limited and potentially dangerous. Sin is a form of 'bad imagination'[19] or wrong seeing. A cursory review of recent history throws up countless examples of heinous imagining: the Final Solution, Hiroshima and Nagasaki, the attack on the Twin Towers, the downing of civilian aeroplanes, ethnic 'cleansing'. Aside from

---

19 Green, *Imagining God*, p. 91.

such public and devastating examples of violent imagination acted out, the imagination can become folded in upon the self, a source of bitter cogitation and plans of petty vengeance. Rooted in faulty perception, imagination can be an agent that leads us to wrong action if we brood on sequences of imagined images of revenge, greed or lust. In essence, practising the divine imagination might be summarized as 'right seeing'. However, the vast gulf between God's imagining and the imagination of the human heart apart from God is clear. We need to have the imprint of the divine imagination pressed upon us again in redemption. The potential for this lies in relationship with Christ 'the image of the invisible God' (Col. 1.15) in and through whom the divine imagination judges, reforms and redeems our broken imagining.

The preacher is not above this broken imagining. Self-interest, insecurity, the need to be liked and needed can all influence our preaching, hence the vital importance for the preacher of opening themselves to the scrutiny of others, be that a spiritual director or soul friend, someone who can help them name false seeing and restore faithful trust in God who alone breathes life into dead words.

Exercising wise *dominion*, in the sense of leadership and care over creation – which might be in any context from family life to farming, mending a car to managing a business, leading a church to preaching a sermon – calls for the exercise of imagination in its various functions: a rich sensory imagination, noticing what needs attention; entrepreneurial intuition, making creative connections; the exercise of affective empathy and sympathy; careful consideration along the 'if . . . then' lines of intellectual hypothesizing. In short, effective 'dominion' calls for wise imagination.

In the Genesis account the command to be 'fruitful and multiply' seems most clearly to mean to *procreate*. There is a similarity between the bringing to birth of a child and the more general human desire to create.

We sense the divine creativity, in a most intimate way, in our own deepest desire – the desire to create, to be radically original, to break through our limitations, to fulfil God's dream in us, to become full of divine light.[20]

Creatio ex nihilo is the work of the imagination of God. In exercising our unique creativity, humanity can only create from that which is given – all our creating is from something. Works of art are created from given materials and, no matter how original, art is always derivative because humanity exists in time, in communities, in relationship and in creation. Literature is coined in words, new words are formed from pre-existing shapes, sounds and categories; all artistic creation is from something. The genius of human imagining is the bringing together of the unusual and the unexpected, rethinking old ideas in new formats. That which is derived from something else can also be 'new', innovative and surprising. Juxtaposing ideas and images in unexpected ways can enable a new seeing of something and therefore a deeper appreciation and learning.

Here the concept of *bricoleur* is useful. A *bricoleur* is an artist who uses the materials around them, which were not necessarily designed for the purpose to which they put them. By adaptation, trial and error, alteration and juxtaposition, they create something new from the old, termed *bricolage*. What can the preacher learn from the concept of *bricolage*? Like Shakespeare's Autolycus, the preacher as *bricoleur* is a 'snapper-up of unconsidered trifles'. The *bricoleur* reflects on whatever comes their way, searching the Scriptures and the world for ideas, images, words, phrases, experiences and stories that can be combined in ways that, illuminated by the revelatory impulse in the sermon-event, might enable a 'new seeing' of God. This capacity to combine and recombine and to create the new from the old is a gift of the intuitive imagination. Preaching is an inherently imaginative undertaking, requiring the imaginative engagement of the preacher in the creation of sermonic material and of the hearer in the shaping of the sermon they hear.

---

20 O'Leary, 'Imagination', p. 525.

God, play and preaching

Imagination has connotations of playfulness and play is a fruitful concept to bring into conversation with preaching. The idea that God plays with creation is inherent in a number of biblical pictures. The Jerusalem Bible translates Psalm 104.26 as follows: 'there ships pass to and fro, and Leviathan whom you made to *sport with*'. This image presents a playful picture of God that resonates with the translation of Proverbs 8.30–31, which describes Wisdom personified:

> I was beside the master craftsman, delighting him day after day, ever at *play* in his presence, at *play* everywhere on his earth, delighting to be with the children of men.[21]

Zechariah 8.5 speaks of the time when God will dwell in Jerusalem and the 'squares of the city will be full of boys and girls playing there'. Play is seen here as an aspect of God's character and community. There is certainly a playfulness in much of Jesus' teaching, most obviously in the parables.

Preaching and play are not words we might naturally associate together; surely preaching is a serious business and play merely an idle pastime? Johan Huizinga describes humans as *homo ludens*, seeing play as basic to culture. In his analysis play is voluntary; there is fun in it; it is a stepping out of 'real' life into a specific location for a certain duration; and within the play there are rules. Even when a game is finished a play-community tends to become permanent. The sense of having been apart together in a particular situation, having withdrawn from the world of the everyday and submitted to the rules of the game, has a bonding effect beyond the play itself. Ritual is a form of play and sacred performances take place in a sacred space, which is 'a temporarily real world of its own'.[22] We can

---

21 Other translations do not use the word 'play'; related terms such as 'delighting' and 'rejoicing' are employed in the AV, NIV and NRSV.

22 Johan Huizinga, *Homo Ludens*, London: Paladin, 1970.

think of 'play' in terms of a to and fro movement. When we play we enter a space and accept certain 'rules' or limitations. All our playing has seriousness about it; a player who enters the game without seriousness spoils the play. There is freedom, spontaneity and open-endedness in play. When we enter into a game the game plays us: 'the game masters the players'.[23]

Applying these ideas about play to preaching we begin to see the potential dynamism of the sermon-event as a game we play. The hearers are no longer passive recipients consigned to the bench. For the sermon to exist at all, the hearers must all be invited into the play. God is the one who invites. The players are free to engage in the play or not; there can be no coercion. The play operates according to certain rules that will vary according to local context. Any preacher who goes over or under the expected time limit is left in no doubt that a rule has been breached! The sermon itself is not the text that the preacher clutches in their sweaty hand. The sermons – for there are always as many sermons as there are hearers – emerge in the to and fro of play that occurs in the space between the preacher, the hearer and the Scripture. In this movement there is the potential to discern the word of God, speaking into our individual situations and shaping us as community. This model sees the power of preaching being exercised by all the players in the Church community. In the game of preaching, the preacher has a particular task. In an earlier stage in the game the biblical text played him, capturing his imagination, producing material that is then shaped and played out in the field of the preaching event. How it is shaped and the way it is played out are imaginative tasks. The task of the players is to enter into a willing suspension of disbelief, a willingness to run with the as-if of the sermon, even if the material is ultimately rejected. The hearer listens for the voice of God present in the play, open to the sacramental potential of the game and following

---

23 Hans-Georg Gadamer, *Truth and Method*, trans. Joel Weinsheimer and Donald G. Marsha, London: Continuum, 2004, pp. 102–10.

the connections that occur as they trace the implications of the preacher's moves on the material of their lives.

Sermons that have no 'play' in them, which assume in their use of language and mode of delivery that the job of the hearer is simply to 'catch the ball', are likely to be resisted in a context that is wary of authority and the misuse of power. The preacher hopes that in the playful event of the sermon the hearers will engage with God and find the resources they need to live out their particular Christian vocation in the days ahead. It is worth recalling that fun is an aspect of play. While it would not be appropriate for all sermons to be fun, at least some of the time the preacher might consider the possibilities of humour in the play of the sermon.

Thinking of 'play' in terms of 'child's play' calls for preachers and hearers to be curious and open-minded, with the innocent and playful outlook of the child, open to wonder, reverence and joy. Becoming an adult can lead to an atrophying of imagination. Jesus' teaching that the kingdom of heaven belongs to such as these[24] underscores the need to stimulate childlike vision, playfulness, trust and joy in and through the preaching event.

In *The Development of Imagination*, David Cohen and Stephen MacKeith helpfully identify stages in imaginative development, pointing to early, simple creative behaviours, such as pretending that an inanimate object is another object; to endowing it with life and creating imaginary companions; holding imaginary conversations and play-acting.[25] Associated with this is joining in with the stories of others, which might be hearing a story, reading a story or producing a play. Participating in another's story is a trait that does not fade with age; it is essential to reading, engaging with news, theatre and film, and it is a skill crucial to preaching, as we join in with the stories of the text, our immediate situation and the wider context. Paul Harris' work on imagination is consonant

---

24 Matt. 19.14; Luke 18.16; Mark 10.14.

25 David Cohen and Stephen A. MacKeith, *The Development of Imagination*, London and New York: Routledge, 1992, pp. 107–9.

with Cohen and MacKeith in regarding imagination as a key part of humanity throughout the life cycle, rather than a childish mode to be outgrown.

> Far from being a peculiarity of childhood, children's susceptibility to emotional engagement in imagined material is a characteristic of the human species throughout the life cycle, rather than a short lived phenomenon of the early years.[26]

Reflecting on the serious nature of play, Harris alerts us to the integrated nature of imagination and cognition, seen even in the very young. In engaging in pretence, children draw from their knowledge of conceptual reality, offering the potential to explore inherent possibilities. To demonstrate this, Harris uses the example of putting a teddy bear in a box, turning on imaginary taps, using a wooden block as soap and giving teddy a bath. In this example he reports that the two-year-old joins in and states that teddy is wet before wrapping him in paper.[27] Here we can clearly see that imaginative play involves both pretence *and* logical, cognitive processes operating at the same time, even in the very young. The child suspends literal interpretation, since teddy is not objectively wet, but is guided by the causal chain of events provided by the narrative framework of the imagining: *if* teddy is put in the bath, and the taps are turned on, and he is washed, *then* he will become wet and need to be dried.

Drawing from a variety of observations,[28] Harris argues that children as young as two and a half to three years are able to engage in role-play, setting aside their own viewpoint and assuming that of the invented person, entering into a simulation and drawing from their knowledge of the world to speak and act in ways appropriate to the adopted role. While

---

26 Paul L. Harris, *The Work of the Imagination: Understanding Children's Worlds*, Oxford: Blackwell, 2000, p. 80.

27 Harris, *Work of the Imagination*, pp. 9–10.

28 Piaget; Miller and Garvey; Dunn and Dale – all cited in Harris, *Work of the Imagination*, p. 31.

the occurrence of such role-play wanes in adulthood, Harris points out that 'we should not mistake an outer decline for an inner change'.[29] He identifies continuities between children and adults around this theme of imaginative pretence, making a link between childhood imaginative play and the adult reading of fiction. Both require the willingness to enter a pretend framework and be governed by the rules of that framework.

Engaging in imaginative play, whether as a child or an adult, seems to have a number of functions and possible outcomes: playfulness, enjoyment, vicarious and affective experience, exploration and cognitive engagement.

> Pretend play is not an activity that is doomed to suppression but the first indication of a lifelong mental capacity to consider alternatives to reality.[30]

It is useful to note here the connection Walter Brueggemann makes between preaching and the 'poetic construal of an alternative world'.[31] This connection suggests that preaching has a seriously playful quality about it, playful in the sense of exploring possibility, asking 'What if?' questions and painting alternative vistas. Such playfulness is serious as it has the potential to render transformation of the self, the community and the wider context.

Recognizing the serious nature of creative playfulness, the imaginative preacher will seek to create sermons that leave space for the hearer to step inside. Tightly woven propositional sermons tend to leave little space for the hearer to enter into the play and engage creatively with God in the shaping of their sermon for that moment in their story. This does not mean that sermons need to look like baggy jumpers full of great holes, rather that the structure needs to allow space in the 'weave'

---

29 Harris, *Work of the Imagination*, p. 36.
30 Harris, *Work of the Imagination*, p. 28.
31 Walter Brueggemann, *Finally Comes the Poet: Daring Speech for Proclamation*, Minneapolis, MN: Fortress Press, 1989, p. 6.

for the hearer to get inside. Sermons full of certainty and overflowing with 'shoulds' and 'oughts' can leave the hearer feeling bulldozed, with no space to explore or object, ponder or wonder.

This chapter has sought to ground the argument for the importance of imagination for preaching in discussion of what the content and form of Scripture suggest about imagination, as well as examining the connection between imagination and some key theological concepts: revelation, incarnation, the divine character and the *imago Dei*. Preaching is an inescapably imaginative act. It is a seriously playful expression of the theology of the Church seeking to connect with the hearers' narrative, by sparking connections in their hearts and minds.

3

Preaching in the Lyrical Voice

Have you ever listened to a sermon and thought, 'Well, yes. Heard that before. And so what difference does it make?' – a sermon that is worthy and orthodox and yet so tedious you could stab yourself; full of cliché and platitude; rammed full of impossible 'shoulds' and 'oughts'. Then there's the sermon with the easy slick answers that simply flattens your objections and leaves you feeling faithless, foolish and voiceless. I've heard some of these and preached my fair share – *mea culpa*. But what about those sermons that cause the heart to catch and the imagination to soar? What about those sermons that somehow seem to bind the individual hearers into a community leaning in to hear more, laughing together, sighing together, nodding in recognition, seeking God together? What about those sermons that ignite the longing of the human heart for something more; those sermons that seem to throw on the spotlights and help you to see anew? Such preaching is laden with transformative potential, alive to the revelatory power of the Word pulsing through our human language. I don't know about you, but I want to preach more of those kinds of sermons – and bury the others in a big hole.

Walter Brueggemann astutely observes that 'reduced speech leads to reduced lives'. He calls for 'alternative modes of speech', speech that is dramatic, artistic, invitational, tensive, prophetic and poetic. In his analysis the language of prose is the language of foreshortened vision in contrast to the insightful nature of poetic language. We might recognize this foreshortened vision in the sermon that closes down the human cry of doubt or confusion, or preaches an easy, cheap form of grace. Of course, prose can be poetic, but Brueggemann is using the term 'prose' to point to the flattened language of 'settled truth' and 'pervasive reductionism'. He points to the preacher as a prophet/poet who comes and shatters the 'dread dullness' of our prose world, which has eviscerated the power of the gospel by trivializing it. Preaching as poetic speech peels back the layers of inanity and tedium and discloses new hope, new vision and new possibility.[1] Brueggemann writes much on the political and spiritual importance of such speech, and his vision does make the heart catch. He often speaks of the imagination in relation to preaching, though he says little about either the nature of imagination or the craft of such preaching. The question remains: how can preachers create such alternative modes of speech? What approaches will help the sermon to sing a new song?

Preaching in the lyrical voice is marked by a desire to grasp the disclosure of the gospel imaginatively and communicate that by drawing from the craft of poetic expression. This chapter offers a description of the hallmarks of lyrical preaching and some analysis of excerpts from sermons crafted in the lyrical voice. At the heart of lyrical preaching is the concern to construct sermons that enable people to 'see' through their ears. This is at the heart of all good radio speech and is essential to effective preaching.

Later in the chapter caveats are entered concerning the limits of language when attempting to speak of the divine. The tools of lyrical preaching are explored in some detail, focusing on analogy, simile and metaphor. The aim throughout is to demonstrate that Brueggemann's vision for alternative modes of speech is met in lyrical preaching and that imaginative engagement is vital in preaching in the lyrical voice.

---

1 Walter Brueggemann, *Finally Comes the Poet: Daring Speech for Proclamation*, Minneapolis, MN: Fortress Press, 1989, pp. 1–11.

What is lyrical preaching?

Preaching in the lyrical voice is *not an argument that sermons should be poems*.

The poet in 'taking wing into realms of daring thought' can 'outsoar the needs and natural expression of the majority of people who compose a typical congregation anywhere'.[2] Speaking of hymnody, David Brown comments that hymns need to appeal to a range of intellects, and given that there is no time for prior reflection on the meaning of the words used, only relatively accessible language can work, 'but this emphatically should not entail the absence of the poetic'.[3] This argument can be applied to preaching. It is quite wrong to assume that poetic language must belong to some special bracketed-off arty world, too rich for the humble diet of everyday speech. A painter does not assume that their most honed artistic techniques and best paints can only be used for high-blown art. Lyrical preaching is not a version of the sermon for high days and holidays. The preacher needs to employ poetic insight and learn from the craft of poetic expression in the everyday, so that sermons, while not poems in themselves, have features of the lyrical about them. Such preaching seeks to be dramatic, artistic, invitational, tensive, prophetic and poetic.

Poetic expression is personal; it seeks to create new contexts for old symbols, minting new metaphors that allow us to see in new ways, inviting contemplation. The impulse behind the struggle to find the right expression is to see more clearly and to enable others to do so, using language to open windows into new vistas of possibility – an inherently imaginative undertaking involving imaginative associations between the word of God and contemporary images. The alternative to such lyrical

---

2 W. E. Sangster, *The Craft of Sermon Illustration*, London: Epworth Press, 1946, p. 79.

3 David Brown, *God and Mystery in Words: Experience through Metaphor and Drama*, Oxford: Oxford University Press, 2008, p. 82.

theology is a 'dead language and a ghettoized Christianity'.[4] The poetic imagination can be a bearer of truth, helping to 'renew and deepen our vision of the world'.[5] Borrowing from the tools of the poet, lyrical preaching is a homiletic strategy that seeks to evoke, intimate, gesture and co-operate with the disclosive impetus of God. It is always seeking to discover the more beyond what we directly experience. To create sermons that lift the 'dread dullness of the prose world' requires sensitivity to biblical language and to the language we use to communicate. The theological attitude underpinning this is a refusal to be satisfied with the easy or glib, a willingness to mine difficult questions and wrestle with paradox, confident that in the struggle God is to be found. Lyrical preaching recognizes the power of language to lift and reshape vision. In the age of the digital, the fast-moving image and the all-pervasive camera, the lyrical voice doggedly champions the disclosive power of the spoken word. At the heart of lyrical preaching is the desire to help people to 'see' through their ears.

Through the ear you see

'A sermon is not an essay to be read but a discourse to be heard . . . directed towards the listening ear rather than the reading eye'.[6] Writing for the ear requires the employment of multisensory language, helping the hearer to imaginatively see, hear, smell, touch and taste the scene. Lyrical preaching can be seen as visual speech, or verbal iconography. It consciously blurs the distinction between spoken word and visual image, using language to help the hearer create their own internal imagery

4 Sallie McFague, *Speaking in Parables: A Study in Metaphor and Theology*, 2nd edn, London: SCM Press, 2002, pp. 83–91.

5 Malcolm Guite, *Faith, Hope and Poetry: Theology and the Poetic Imagination*, Farnham: Ashgate, 2012, pp. 1, 5, 15, 243.

6 Martin Luther King Jr, *Strength to Love*, New York: Harper & Row, 1963, pp. ix–x, in Mervyn A. Warren, *King Came Preaching*, Downers Grove, IL: InterVarsity Press, 2001, pp. 151–2.

as they draw from the sensory input of the sermon. Preaching, like radio speech, can 'fire imagination with pictorial language'. Such pictorial and experiential language has the potential to create 'alternative imaginative worlds for listeners'.[7] The following extract from a radio report by American war correspondent Ed Murrow, master of the 'little picture', highlights the effectiveness of description that attends to detail. Can you imagine the scene Murrow is depicting? What can you see? What do you hear? What feelings does the description evoke?

> One night last week I stood in front of a smashed grocery store and heard a dripping inside. It was the only sound in all London. Two cans of peaches had been drilled through by flying glass and the juice was dripping down onto the floor.[8]

Analysing this, we see/hear that the focus on the sound of the peach juice 'dripping', an example of the effective use of onomatopoeia.[9] This, combined with the hyperbolic[10] statement that this was 'the only sound in London', creates a haunting and evocative effect. The reporter effectively creates a visual 'close up' on the drops of syrup. The sense of violence is captured in the verb 'drilling' and the reference to 'flying glass'. With a breathtaking economy of words, the reporter paints a sense of destruction and waste without overdescribing the scene.

On the basis of his research into radio speech, Jolyon Mitchell offers four imperatives to the preacher: to listen, picture, translate and edit.[11] He recommends 'multi-faceted listening': listening to the context; the congregation; the theological issues

---

7 Jolyon Mitchell, *Visually Speaking: Radio and the Renaissance of Preaching*, Edinburgh: T. & T. Clark, 1999, pp. 20, 6.

8 Mitchell, *Visually Speaking*, p. 52.

9 Onomatopoeia is a technique in which the writer uses a word that sounds like the sound it describes, e.g. 'thumping', 'squealing', 'tapping'.

10 Hyperbole means exaggeration for effect.

11 Mitchell, *Visually Speaking*, pp. 223–34.

raised in popular culture; the nature of everyday language; the musicality of words themselves and the acoustic environment of scriptural narrative. We might add to this the need for deep listening for the whisper of God. This kind of deep listening requires the sensing imagination to be on high alert. As we saw in the example above, picturing effectively in language calls for description that allows the hearer space to step into the discourse and imaginatively appropriate the scene for themselves. Too many adjectives 'clutter oral language and prevent communication'.[12] Sensitive to this danger the lyrical preacher will rely on nouns and verbs as the tools of description.[13] Mitchell reminds the preacher of the importance of avoiding religious jargon, advocating the translation of biblical and theological terms into vivid, conversational language. It falls to the intuitive function of imagination to forge such language, alert to connections between the abstract theological concept and the concrete example. Mitchell's final imperative for the preacher is to edit: a process involving the removal of redundant expression, which Richard Eslinger memorably calls 'empty-calorie language'. He offers a number of examples: overused adverbs such as 'truly', 'very' or 'really'; phrases such as 'if only we would', 'if only we might', 'I just want . . . '; sloppy fillers such as 'you know', 'well' and 'like'.[14] Conversational sermon language is not sloppy or ill conceived, it is carefully crafted and delivered, however relaxed and informal it might be in tone.

What are the hallmarks of the lyrical sermon?

While not every sermon will demonstrate all these features, many of them will be discernible in the lyrical sermon. Use the

---

12 David Buttrick, *Homiletic Moves and Structures*, Philadelphia: Fortress Press, 1987, p. 192.

13 Richard Eslinger, *Pitfalls in Preaching*, Grand Rapids, MI: Eerdmans, 1996, p. 11.

14 Eslinger, *Pitfalls in Preaching*, p. 15.

columns to the right to tick any features you identify in the example sermon extracts offered below.

	Example 1 x	Example 2 X
Attends to detail of the Scriptures with full sensing imagination		
Sensitive to the genre of Scripture		
Alive to the resonances of Scripture; may weave in Scripture from other biblical sources		
Attends to nouns and verbs to paint vivid pictures		
Makes use of imagery – employing a variety of analogy, metaphor and simile		
Weaves such imagery into the flow of conversational language		
Layers description for cumulative effect		
Alert to context, draws on observation of the everyday to offer instances, or earthed examples, of more abstract ideas		
Uses repetition to powerful effect		
Alive to the possibilities of contrast, e.g. the use of bathos[15] and hyperbole		
Employs the musicality of language, e.g. onomatopoeia and alliteration[16]		

15 Bathos is a poetic technique that juxtaposes the lofty with the commonplace for particular effect.

16 In alliteration, adjacent words that begin with the same sound can contribute to a playful sense of rhythm.

Considers the power of rhythm in spoken word		
Varies sentence length for punchy effect		
Engages affective imagination and stands in the shoes of biblical characters and hearers		
Draws on observation of the everyday to offer instances, or earthed examples, of more abstract ideas		
Alive to the interrelatedness of sermon form and content		

Although this cannot be assessed in a printed sermon extract, the lyrical preacher will ensure that content and delivery support each other, giving consideration to the performative aspects of preaching: vocal intonation, volume, pace, gesture, movement around the space and eye movement and contact. The first extract includes some brief notes relating to this to give a sense to the reader of how the preacher needs to embody the words they preach and inhabit the preaching space, bringing the two-dimensional words off the page and into three-dimensional life. This may raise the objection that preaching is being turned into performance. However, the truth is that all preaching is performative, which is not the same as saying that the preacher is pretending. When we speak of performance we generally mean doing something in a public context. Whether the preacher stands stock still and reads out in a monotone from a script, or inhabits the words with freedom and spontaneity, they are still performing. The question is not to perform or not to perform but *how* to perform such that the sermon is embodied faithfully in a way that helps the hearer to enter into the experience.

Example 1 – an extract from a sermon based on Luke 8.22–39

As you read it, try to identify hallmarks of preaching in the lyrical voice using the checklist above.

> First let's zoom in on the disciples after the storm has been stilled.
> *[use eye line, gesture and hand movement to indicate the disciples' position in the body of the preaching space]*
> There they are, hair plastered down by lake water, crouching in a half-submerged boat, its hull caressed by gentle wavelets. For all the calm around them, in their hearts and minds they are buffeted by questions: fear, awe, wonder. Perhaps a tempest of recrimination blasts at them? They have woken up to their spiritual amnesia.
>
> Peter – had you forgotten so soon?
> *[looking towards the imagined Peter]*
> You saw the nets breaking as the fish slapped into the boat.
> You recognized Jesus as Holy, as Lord.
> You saw him heal people. You heard him teach.
> You were there at Nain when he told the dead man to get up, and he did.
>
> *[turn from Peter to congregation]*
> No, I don't think the calm on the lake is matched by calm in the disciples' hearts:
>
> *[for each question/statement, alter head movement to represent a different speaking voice]*
> 'How could we have been so stupid?'
> 'How could we have forgotten?'
> 'Where is our faith?'
> 'He stands before us – he has power over the elements.'
> 'Here is God with us.'

Jesus the storm bringer
[turn from disciples to congregation]
And what of us? Are we immune to this spiritual amnesia?
Have you had those moments of an intense sense of God,
times when you have prayed and seen God at work?
That mountaintop view that overwhelmed you with awe?
That catchy refrain in a song that spoke straight into your situation?
Sitting in the sublime beauty of a quiet cathedral, infused with a sense of presence?
A moment with a mentor or friend when you suddenly saw that what looked like death is a gateway to life?

Perhaps you write your experience in a journal and come across it sometime later and you are surprised by the memory.
'*How could I have forgotten this?*'
The tensions, trivialities and traumas of life have robbed you.
The banality of life numbed you in its routine.
Spiritual amnesia.
It shrinks Jesus down until he is dashboard-sized.
[use forefinger and thumb to indicate this shrinkage]
We forget – the Lord of heaven and earth,
God almighty, *[looking up, big gesture]*
is only a heartbeat away. *[gesture coming in close]*
Where is our faith?
Sometimes we need a storm to wake us up.

Jesus is a storm bringer
He brings a tempest of realization that tears up our self-reliance,
uproots our pint-sized idols . . .[17]

---

17 The full script of this sermon can be found in the Appendix.

Analysis

The piece is written for the ear, seeking to create a multisensory experience in words, showing awareness of the way words and phrases can be layered to resonate and contrast for particular effects. A series of strong visual images creates a sense of context. Stormy images such as 'hair plastered down', 'crouching in a half-submerged boat', 'buffeted by questions', 'tempest of recrimination blasts', 'we need a storm to wake us up' and 'uproots our pint-sized idols' contrast with the calmer imagery of 'hull caressed by gentle wavelets', 'all the calm around them' and 'calm on the lake'.

The metaphor of Jesus as a storm bringer, which was repeated at the end of each move throughout the whole sermon, helped to connect the events on the lake with the 'storm' Jesus creates in the Gerasene region. It also generates tension, pulling away from the commonplace and overworked homiletic decision to preach a sermon on the Christ who calms our storms.

The layering of examples of Jesus' power resonates with the language of 'Lord of heaven and earth' and seeks to generate imaginative shock through juxtaposing such description with the metaphor of Jesus as 'dashboard-sized' and of our 'pint-sized idols'. Such bathos highlights the ludicrous effects of our spiritual amnesia. The inflated language of 'the Lord of heaven and earth, God almighty' is juxtaposed with the image 'only a heartbeat away', underscoring a sense of transcendence embracing immanence. God is with us.

The preacher attends to the onomatopoeic potential of language to create a sensory experience in the image of 'fish slapped into the boat' and shows a playful awareness of the musicality of alliteration in the reference to the 'tensions, trivialities and traumas' of life.

Textual context has been carefully considered. Using the techniques of the movie script,[18] the sermon begins with a close-up

---

18 Thomas H. Troeger, *Ten Strategies for Preaching in a Multi-media Culture*, Nashville, TN: Abingdon Press, 1996, pp. 48–59; Buttrick, *Homiletic Moves and Structures*, 1987, pp. 55–68.

on the disciples in the boat, their misery framed. This is followed with stills of Peter's previous experience of Jesus earlier in Luke's narrative. The questioning of Peter's forgetfulness is an imaginative move that roots the sermon firmly within the narrative flow of Luke's account, looking back to previous examples of the revelation of Jesus' power, before we overhear the imagined inner dialogue of the disciples.

The sermon then moves to addressing the hearer directly with potential instances of spiritual connection and our tendency to 'spiritual amnesia'. In this example the preacher has sought to apply the tools of the poet to the task of preaching, seeking to discover the lyrical voice.

Example 2 – an extract from a sermon on Ezekiel 37

What aspects of preaching in the lyrical voice are used here? Use the checklist above. Read the extract aloud. How could you use pace, pause, varied volume and vocal intonation, gesture and eye movement to bring this off the page?

We step out into an eerie scene –
hot and quiet.
Still, deathly still.

On the bleached white sea on which you stand you pick out skulls, tibias, fibulas, jaw bones, tarsals, metatarsals, ribs, spines, ulnas, phalanges, you spot the odd kneecap here and there.
Bleached bones, many in number.

A catastrophe has occurred. The dead are dishonoured.
They have had no burial, but have been picked clean by scavengers.
Bones. Bones. Bones.
Bones under your feet.

Bones as far as your eye can see.
Bones crunching underfoot.
This is death valley.

I don't know about you, but I don't like it here.

So, what does death valley symbolize?
The bones represent the whole house of Israel.
As a people in exile they are dead men and women,
there is no future for the exiles.
They say, '*Our bones are dried up and our hope is lost, we
are cut off completely.*' They have lost their homeland, their
homes.
They are separated from the temple, from Jerusalem,
– both of which will soon be utterly destroyed.
Far from all that is familiar and secure.

It must seem they are far, far, far from God.
Ezekiel is literally and metaphorically preaching to the dead.

Can you hear the words of Psalm 137, playing in the background?
'*By the rivers of Babylon, where we sat down,
there we wept, as we remembered Zion . . .
How can we sing the* LORD'*s song in a strange land?*'
This is the soundtrack to our scene.

Standing amid this sea of bleached dry bones, faced with the
question,
'*Mortal, can these bones live,*' we might be tempted to say:
'*Not a chance. Are you mad? They are bones!*'
Really, the situation is utterly hopeless.
Quite beyond help.

But God . . .
But with God nothing is ever utterly hopeless.
But God . . .

God can do a new thing – even in situations of apparent futility.
God commands Ezekiel to speak to the bones,
to speak into the place of death.
God includes Ezekiel as his agent in his new work.
God uses people, works with people to bring the message of life,
even though only divine initiative can transform the death of exile.
Only God can redeem and restore.

Ezekiel prophesies
and our eerie scene is transformed
into one that is bizarre, wonderful, even comical.
'Suddenly there was a noise, a rattling, and the bones came together, bone to its bone.'

Skulls seeking jawbones, tibias linking with fibulas,
tarsals marrying metatarsals,
ribs and spines, hips and femurs rattling about,
kneecaps flying through the air.
Click, clack, rattle – bones are on the move.[19]

Analysis

The opening three lines of the extract see the preacher sketching out a sense of the scene with an economy of words, inviting the hearers together to 'step out' imaginatively into Ezekiel's vision and feel the heat, hear the silence and experience the bony barrenness of the scene. The metaphor of 'bleached white sea' evokes a grotesque sense of a vast expanse of bones. Identifying types of bone makes the scene more graphic and

---

19 The full script of this sermon can be found in the Appendix.

underscores the sense of deathly hopelessness. This is a move faithful to the drive of the biblical text. The horror is deliberately undercut with the throwaway line 'you spot the odd kneecap here and there'. The sheer volume of bones asserts itself again in the repetition of the word 'bones' and the onomatopoeic reference to the 'crunch underfoot'. Naming this place as 'death valley' overlays images of the real Death Valley, arid and apparently barren and conveys resonances of the valley of the shadow of death from Psalm 23, with its underlying message of hope. Some hearers will pick up these resonances and some will simply run with the melodic line of the unfolding sermon. This does not matter; it simply opens up the potential for a richer hearing for some without losing those who miss these echoes. The lyrical voice is able to communicate in multilayered polyphony.

Having established a sense of large-scale catastrophe the preacher references the exile, using the opening section of Psalm 137 to illustrate a sense of the exiles' grief. Into this situation comes the divine voice, addressed now not to Ezekiel but to preacher and hearer. The apparent futility of hope is underscored by the preacher giving voice to human doubt in the face of the seemingly impossible, using three pithy responses: '*Not a chance. Are you mad? They are bones!*'

The sermon turns on the phrase 'But God', which opens up the potential for a multilayered hearing of the sermon. On one level the ensuing message of hope in deathly places refers to the biblical narrative. Under the divine initiative the bones take on flesh and life comes back, a symbol of hope for the future of the exiles in Babylon. On another level the preacher is inviting the hearer to overlay their 'situations of apparent futility' onto Ezekiel's valley and to find hope in the God who redeems and restores.

An extract from the biblical text is wrapped into the sermon: '*Suddenly there was a noise, a rattling, and the bones came together, bone to its bone.*' The preacher takes time to dwell on this scene, playing with the bizarre images of bones linking together as death is undone. The line 'click, clack, rattle – bones are on the move', being rhythmic in nature, is both memorable and humorous.

The presumption of language

Objections to such preaching may be that it presumes too much for the power of the spoken word. However, underpinning lyrical preaching is a theological consideration of the limits of language as well as its potential to reveal something new. There is a frequent caution in the early fathers over claiming too much for human language. Clement of Alexandria writes that, even in union with Christ, 'we only reach in a measure to the conception of God, knowing not what He is, but what He is not'.[20] Similarly, Origen indicates that the superiority of God renders him beyond the power of unaided human understanding.[21] Hilary of Poitiers reminds us of the difficulty of discovering adequate language for the Divine, a difficulty summed up by John of Damascus when he writes that God 'in His essence and nature is absolutely incomprehensible and unknowable'.[22] There seems to be a stark choice here: complete silence or the attempt, however inadequately, to speak. Augustine observes:

> And yet God, although nothing worthy of His greatness can be said of Him, has condescended to accept the worship of men's mouths, and has desired us through the medium of our own words to rejoice in His praise.[23]

However inadequate our language is, God desires it. In worship, we address God and describe God, offering our praise,

---

20 Ian T. Ramsey, *Words About God*, London: SCM Press, 1971, p. 16.
21 Ramsey, *Words About God*, p. 16.
22 Ramsey, *Words About God*, p. 18.
23 Augustine, *De Doctrina Christiana*, Bk 1, ch. 6, www.georgetown.edu/faculty/jod/augustine/ddc1.html.

penitence, plea, lament and love. Preaching is a part of this act of worship, in which the preacher offers the best of their linguistic skill in an act of service to God transcendent and God immanent in the Church, conscious of the limits of language but trusting in the revelation of God.

Another objection to preaching in the lyrical voice is that it is overly concerned with evoking feelings – touchy-feely language at its worst! However, there is much more to the lyrical voice than the evocation of feeling. Lyrical preaching brings together non-cognitive and cognitive dimensions of religious language. Non-cognitive religious language is concerned with evoking experience, using language artistically to bring delight, to surprise and sometimes to shock. In such non-cognitive understandings, religious language points us not outward towards an objective reality but back towards ourselves. In this perspective preaching might be seen as a cathartic opportunity, an art form, or an encouragement to engage in forms of ethical behaviour. Lyrical preaching can be all of these things – but it is *much* more than this. Lyrical preaching also uses language cognitively to point us towards an objective reality. It stands on the rock of the self-revealing God. We dare to attempt to speak of God because, in Christ, God speaks to us and in Christ our broken words are healed and addressed to God. Preaching in the lyrical voice is grounded in an approach that claims that our words about God, while they can never be finally definitive, do have referential and disclosive potential *because* God is objectively real and is the one who speaks first.

We can experience 'imaginative shock' in that moment when what we thought we knew and understood undergoes rapid revision, reality is redescribed and a new world of possibility is revealed.[24] This concept of imaginative shock lies close to the experience of a disclosure situation in which there is a revelation of depth, the 'light dawns', the 'ice breaks' and the 'penny

---

24 Edward Riegert, *Imaginative Shock: Preaching and Metaphor*, Burlington, Ontario: Trinity Press, 1990, p. 10.

drops'.[25] In such a disclosure the transcendent more of God is revealed through the ordinary discourse of language; the Word incarnate in words.

Disclosure situations consist of two elements: discernment and commitment. Discernment lies in recognizing the 'more' of the disclosure. Commitment involves appreciating the inherent value of that new thing, whether that is a revelation of divine love or the experience of falling in love and having the vision to realign our commitments accordingly. Preaching in the lyrical voice, while recognizing the limitations of language, seeks the response of discernment and commitment in the hearers.

The importance of analogy, simile and metaphor

Analogy

Analogy works by showing the similarity between two things. In this sense, it has affinities with simile and metaphor and there is an overlap between these categories. Often analogy compares an unknown object to something with which we are familiar to help us develop understanding. Janet Soskice comments that 'analogy as a linguistic device deals with language that has been stretched to fit new applications'. While she regards analogy as working with minimal 'imaginative strain',[26] analogy can create an imaginative jolt in the hearer when the source that is stretched to describe God is unusual or unexpected. Many of the parables create analogies between humans and God and then invert our expectations by having the human character act outside the expectations of the analogy, throwing new light on our understanding of God. For example, stretching human categories and applying them to God initially seems to suggest that God, like fathers, should

25 Ian T. Ramsey, *Religious Language*, London: SCM Press, 1957, p. 19.
26 Janet Martin Soskice, *Metaphor and Religious Language*, Oxford: Clarendon Press, 1985, p. 64.

punish errant children; like bosses should pay people according to productivity; like a gardener should attend to weeding. In all three parables the expectation in the analogical stretch is inverted.[27] Such parables operate with analogical power because they highlight difference in the similarity.

There are pitfalls in using analogy to speak of God. Any univocal connections between the human and the divine will lead to anthropomorphism. This may result from a failure to specify that if we speak, say, of God's love we need to qualify in what ways divine love is *unlike* human love. In preaching, too close an analogical connection between the human and the divine may result in a negative response. If God is described through the analogy of human love and the hearer's knowledge of human love is that it is fickle, unreliable and ever shifting, the analogy, without further qualification, is likely to lead to a negative view of God. The preacher needs to imagine and address the contrapuntal that their analogies might give rise to in the hearer.

However, if language about humans is used equivocally of God then we cannot really describe God positively at all. If God's love is *nothing* like human love, then the analogy has no descriptive power. As Astley points out, our God-talk needs to walk the tightrope between the univocal and the equivocal.[28] In spite of its epistemological limitations, Paul Avis maintains that analogy is 'a serviceable tool of unpretentious theological work, in preaching, catechizing and biblical interpretation'. He sees the usefulness of analogies which, with elaboration and refinement, can become building blocks of theological construction. For example, he takes the metaphor of kingship and draws from it the analogy between earthly kingship and God's rule, showing how an analogical form can be developed from this while highlighting the importance of critical scrutiny and careful elucidation of the similarities and differences between

---

27 Luke 15.1–32; Matt. 13.24–30; 20.1–16.
28 Jeff Astley, *Exploring God-talk: Using Language in Religion*, London: Darton, Longman & Todd, 2004, pp. 57–8.

divine and human government.[29] Analogical language functions with the tension between 'is' and 'is not' that is also characteristic of simile and metaphor.

Simile

There is some disagreement in the literature concerning the power and potential of simile. A simile compares one thing with another to throw light on that which is being described, hinging on the words 'as' or 'like'. It is often seen as the poorer cousin to metaphor and lacking deep descriptive power. One argument is that in simile the shock in the comparison is reduced by the word 'like', which screens out dissimilarity and collapses the tension between the 'is' and 'is not' that metaphor supplies.[30]

Is simile simply about making comparison, lacking deep descriptive power? To what extent is the presence of 'as' or 'like' a mere grammatical detail or even an impediment to deeper meaning? Janet Soskice helpfully champions the power of the simile by differentiating between 'illustrative similes' and 'modelling similes'.[31] The illustrative simile takes two things that are known and uses one to give a sense of the other; for example, 'as fast as a hare', 'as ferocious as a bear'. The scope of such similes is limited, in contrast to the potential of the modelling simile which, like metaphor, potentially takes us beyond our first cognitive grasp on a subject, into new territory.

Modelling similes take something known and use it to open up and develop cognitive apprehension of something beyond our grasp. For example, the writer of Hosea 13.8 uses the following simile: 'I will fall upon them like a bear robbed of her

---

29 Paul Avis, *God and the Creative Imagination: Metaphor, Symbol and Myth in Religion and Theology*, London: Routledge, 1999, pp. 73, 76–7.

30 Sallie McFague, *Metaphorical Theology: Models of God in Religious Language*, Philadelphia: Fortress Press, 1982, p. 38.

31 Soskice, *Metaphor and Religious Language*, p. 59.

cubs, and will tear open the covering of their heart.' This simile takes something known – the fury of a mother bear whose cubs have been taken – to illustrate something unknown, in this case the nature of the relationship between God and his people. God's rage with the rebellion of Israel is like that of a mother bear robbed of her cubs. At the same time it is those cubs whom she threatens to attack and rip open. The simile holds together both the righteous fury of God and a subtle underlying message of hope in the maternal image offered for God. In Matthew 23.37 and Luke 13.34, Jesus is imaged as a mother hen in the lament over Jerusalem. This simile also operates with metaphoric power, offering a startling model for Christ's love for the people of Jerusalem. The simile portrays Christ as protective, maternal and nurturing, offering warmth and comfort. As a corollary, the people are imaged as clucking chickens, running away from their source of protection because they were not willing to accept him. Soskice's distinction between illustrative and modelling similes is helpful for the preacher. A modelling simile extends beyond simple illustration and opens up the potential for deeper exploration of meaning and resonance.

Metaphor

As we shall see, metaphor has the power to enable new ways of seeing and, potentially, new ways of acting in the world. Given this, preachers need to be trained to understand, apprehend, challenge and shape metaphor. The word *metapherō*, constructed from the words *meta* ('with', 'after') and *pherō* ('I carry'), gives us a sense of something being carried over or transferred and links with the broad sense of metaphor as being associated with the idea of a transfer from one thing to another.[32] The employment of metaphor involves 'spotting the

---

32 Astley, *Exploring God-talk*, p. 37.

thread of similarity between two dissimilar objects'[33] or experiencing one thing in terms of another.

Many people think that metaphor is merely ornamental, a kind of special inflated frilly language that has nothing to do with the workaday world of words. However, it is hard to conceive of an example in which metaphor might operate in a purely ornamental way. Compare the following:

> Statement: 'There is smoke coming under the door.'
> Metaphor: 'There is smoke creeping under the door.'

The only difference between the two is the substitution of the verb 'creeping' for 'coming' in the metaphor. Is this merely an ornamental flourish? On the contrary, the verb brings the smoke alive, personifying it as an insidious crafty being, raising a sense of fear and foreboding and creating a strong visual image of the smoke. Even if we seek very simple metaphors that could be expressed similarly in literal terms, it is plain that the metaphor adds further cognitive content. For example, compare:

> Statement: 'She is very pale.'
> Metaphor: 'Her face is drip-white.'

Even this weak metaphor carries cognitive resonances supplied by the intercourse of meaning between the words 'drip-white' and 'face'. In the stripped-down statement the resonances of thinness, weakness, vapidity and shock are lost. We are left with just a pale-faced woman; the removal of the metaphor has robbed the line of cognitive content, bearing out this point:

---

33 McFague, *Metaphorical Theology*, p. 15.

The relevant weakness of the literal paraphrase is not that it may be tiresomely prolix or boringly explicit (or deficient in qualities of style); it fails to be a translation because it fails to give the insight that the metaphor did.[34]

Similarly, take the metaphor 'He is a fox'. To convey the same cognitive content would take a wide variety of literal statements, as many as there are interpretations and nuances relating to the word 'fox': he is cunning, wily, a scavenger, predatory, he hunts at night, he is attractive and so on. These simple examples show clearly that metaphor can never be seen as merely decorative.

Understood as merely decorative, metaphor has excited criticism from the empiricist perspective. In his *Essay Concerning Human Understanding*,[35] John Locke warns that figurative speech, while bringing delight, is misleading: a serious charge for the lyrical preacher who wishes to develop the use of metaphor. The argument runs that figurative language is to be avoided on the grounds that the metaphoric, in exciting affective response, misleads judgement. But why should the generation of affect be misleading? We could argue that an emotional response to an issue can inform judgement. Indeed, if a sermon is to move the will, then it needs to ignite the heart as well as appeal to the mind. That aside, in this perspective literal truth is presented as being superior to metaphoric meaning. For Locke, the plain truth should be spoken plainly. This view implies that there is a category of language that might be termed direct, as opposed to the 'misleading' indirection of metaphor.

However, metaphor is embedded in language and shapes our concept systems. This view effectively counters the idea of metaphor as a substitution for a more literal means of saying

---

34 Max Black, *Models and Metaphors: Studies in Language and Philosophy*, Ithaca, NY: Cornell University Press, 1962, p. 46.

35 John Locke, *Essay Concerning Human Understanding*, Vol. II, Oxford: Clarendon Press, 1894, pp. 146–7; see also Soskice, *Metaphor and Religious Language*, pp. 12–13.

something. The point is perhaps most succinctly made in relation to the exploration of the metaphor 'time is money'. We commonly speak of time in terms such as: wasting, saving, spending, costing, having, budgeting, investing, offering and losing.[36] In another example we can identify a range of words and phrases that suggest the governing conceptual metaphor of life as a gambling game. We use such terms as: odds, playing an ace, playing your cards right, high stakes, bluffing, 'the luck of the draw' and the 'chips are down'.[37] Along with such governing conceptual metaphors we use orientational metaphors that are culturally embedded.[38] Happy is generally 'up' and sad is 'down'; we might speak of spirits being boosted or lifted, energy levels soaring, a mood rising; or of feeling down, depressed or low. Consciousness is portrayed with up words and unconsciousness with down language: we wake up and get up but fall asleep, drop off and go under anaesthetic. Within our culture more is up and less is down, so we speak of income rising, unemployment soaring, turning the volume up, having high status and of markets taking a downturn, of losing income and so forth. What is crucially important is that these governing metaphors are part of our everyday thought and language: we use them 'unconsciously and automatically, with so little effort that we hardly notice'.[39] Far from being a matter of ornament, metaphor is deeply embedded in language.

The power of metaphor in public speech, operating far beyond mere ornamentation, is well demonstrated in the following example. It occurs in the context of a court hearing in which a large firm was defending a suit from a smaller one and apparently winning.

---

36 George Lakoff and Mark Johnson, *Metaphors We Live By*, Chicago: University of Chicago Press, 1980, pp. 7–9.

37 Lakoff and Johnson, *Metaphors We Live By*, p. 51.

38 Lakoff and Johnson, *Metaphors We Live By*, pp. 14–21.

39 George Lakoff and Mark Turner, *More than Cool Reason: A Field Guide to Poetic Metaphor*, London: University of Chicago Press, 1989, p. xi.

> Then the lawyer for the small utility said, speaking to the jury, almost as if incidentally to his legal case, 'So now we see what it is. They got us where they want us. They holding us up with one hand, their good sharp fishin' knife in the other, and they sayin', "you jes set still, little catfish, we're jes going to gut ya"'.[40]

The use of the dramatic metaphor, linking a small company with a little catfish and depicting the larger company as a hunter, carries powerful inferences of butchery, bullying and injustice. The brutality is underscored with reference to 'good sharp fishin' knife' and the declaration 'we're jes going to gut ya'. This, combined with the colloquial language and vivid, contextually relevant imagery, enabled the jury to see the matter in a new light. The penny drops and reality is redescribed in a moment of powerful disclosure: metaphor has much more than mere ornamental function.

Metaphor: the interanimation of words

One of the criticisms of metaphor is its vagueness. If we say that 'Tom is a wolf', with the common descriptors associated with wolves left unstated yet implicit, we are left with the problem of knowing in what way Tom is a wolf. And how are we to know what is entailed by the sun in the metaphor 'Juliet is the sun'? It might mean '"Juliet is for the most part gaseous" or "Juliet is a million miles from the earth"'.[41] This is a fair point, but we need to attend to the 'interanimation of words', conscious that we arrive at meaning through the whole utterance and its surrounding context rather than through words in

---

40 Wayne Booth, 'Metaphor as Rhetoric: The Problem of Evaluation', *Critical Enquiry* 5:1 (1978), p. 52.

41 John R. Searle, 'Metaphor', in *Metaphor and Thought*, ed. Andrew Ortony, Cambridge: Cambridge University Press, 1979, p. 106.

isolation.[42] If we see metaphor as embedded in a larger text and context, this reduces the range of possible entailments. Given that Romeo utters the words at sunrise, as the woman he loves comes to her window, at the opening of a speech that develops a metaphor of Juliet in terms of heavenly light, it seems clear that the context limits the range of possible interpretations. The fact that there are a range of possible interpretations that combine, within a limited field, to illustrate the nature of Romeo's love underscores the rich, fertile potential of metaphor. The lyrical preacher will be attuned to the interanimation of words, images and sentences throughout the sermon.

Metaphor: the theological importance of transference

In the metaphor 'man is a wolf', the principal element is 'man' since this is the focal point of the metaphor. 'Wolf' is the subsidiary element, used to help us gain understanding of 'man'. It is important to note that the transference of ideas associated with man and wolf occurs in both directions:

> If to call a man a wolf is to put him in a special light, we must not forget that the metaphor makes the wolf seem more human than he otherwise would.[43]

This is a particularly important point for the preacher since in any metaphor describing God our understanding of the subsidiary element in the metaphor is also modified. Take the metaphor 'God is father'. The transference moves in both directions – our understanding of God is potentially opened up and so is our understanding of fatherhood, which is elevated both in terms of our expectation of what a father should be and in terms of the potential for actions committed in the name of fatherhood to be divinized. Metaphors for God have the power

---

42 I. A. Richards, *Philosophy of Rhetoric*, New York: Oxford University Press, 1965, p. 55.

43 Black, *Models and Metaphors*, p. 44.

to give us new insights into the nature of God and to reveal to us our attitudes towards the subsidiary subjects we might use to enable a new vision of God.

Most useful for the preacher is the point that metaphors function in speech communities with shared assumptions and beliefs. Where those commonplaces do not exist, metaphors break down. Thus to describe God as shepherd in a context where the concept of shepherd has few shared commonplaces is to offer an ineffective metaphor. The implications for preachers are clear: they need to forge new metaphors *and* find ways of reinvigorating the old metaphors. If people are to engage with the richness of biblical metaphors, there is a need to create shared associations of commonplaces. This is one of the tasks of developing biblical literacy: increasing people's cognitive and emotional familiarity with the key biblical metaphors. Preachers also need to attend carefully to their means of communication outside the speech community of the Church, finding metaphors that convey the gospel in a culture that does not share the associated commonplaces of a biblical worldview.

Poets and writers can create 'specially constructed systems of implications' to support metaphors:

> But in a poem or a piece of sustained prose [or a sermon], the writer can establish a novel pattern of implications for the literal uses of key expressions, prior to using them as vehicles for metaphors.[44]

This, too, is an important point for the preacher. To illustrate, in working to communicate a sense of the meaning of 'life from death' the preacher could draw from a pool of contextual and cultural commonplaces drawn from literal usage, so as to create a pattern of associations that begin to elucidate potential meanings for a concept difficult to convey – for example: the football club that avoids relegation; the unemployed person who finds work; the regeneration of industry; the all-clear after

---

44 Black, *Models and Metaphors*, p. 43.

a cancer scare. These instances create a series of associations with the concept of new possibilities in a situation of apparent hopelessness. The cognitive and emotive force of these associations can then be drawn on when exploring the biblical metaphor of life from death.

Metaphor: bearer of subtle implication

Metaphor can create subtle implications communicated by inference rather than direct statement. Look at the following extract from a sermon.[45]

> I looked out of the window of my flat and found myself captivated by a scene unfolding on the pavement below. I saw a young girl, about six years old, tottering along on the pavement in a pair of her mother's red, high-heeled shoes. The child looked so pleased with herself, proud to be in her mother's shoes, in spite of the fact she kept falling over as she tottered along. The child's joy and determination were wonderful to watch. As I pondered the scene, I became aware of a strong sense of God. You know that feeling? The divine nudge in the ribs? I wondered. Was there a connection between my delight at the little girl's attempts to walk in her mother's shoes and God's response as we try to 'walk in God's shoes'?

The metaphor communicates some interesting implications that were never made explicit in the telling of the story. The implicit image is of God as mother, and a particular kind of mother: one who does not intervene when her children fall over in the process of learning, who is not critical and who observes the attempts of her child to imitate her with pleasure and approval. Had the preacher directly introduced the idea of the maternal in God it is likely that some would have closed

---

45 From a sermon given by the Revd Canon Di Johnson.

down the possibility because of being theologically and culturally conditioned into only ascribing the masculine to God. The metaphor functioned well in the sermon since it created a sense of warmth and invitation to consider the implications of the story, and it also revealed to us something of the spirituality and character of the preacher, generating a willingness to listen seriously to what they wanted to communicate.

This example points up the need for a variety of metaphors in our preaching since this metaphor alone portrays humanity as children, which implicitly reduces the degree of responsibility we hold for our failure to walk appropriately in the divine path.

All attempts to explain the nature and relations of the deity must largely depend on metaphor, and no one metaphor can exhaust those relations. Each metaphor can only describe one aspect of the nature and being of the deity and the inferences that can be drawn from it have their limits when they conflict with the inferences that can be drawn from other metaphors describing other aspects.[46]

Thus if God is king, lord and potentate he is so in a fatherly way, as a protective shepherd or a fierce mother bear. This riotous mixing of metaphors reflects the imaginative creativity of the biblical writers and calls forth all the imaginative ingenuity of the preacher. Preachers need to adopt a wide range of images for God, thinking creatively of new metaphors and challenging the built-in assumptions of old ones. 'In pulling against one another, rival metaphors can then help generate a better balance.'[47]

Metaphoric language stands as a guard against the human will to power, which wants to close down and control with flattening, fixed statements. The imaginative eye will always note that there is more to be said and more to be said in better ways. Metaphor leaves room for mystery and at the same time invites encounter with that mystery: the encounter of

---

46 Ramsey, *Religious Language*, p. 164.
47 Brown, *God and Mystery in Words*, p. 96.

disclosure, discernment, commitment and faith. Hence figurative language is not merely useful to the sermon, it is essential:

> The power of metaphorical language is awesome. With metaphor we can form attitudes, emotions, and profound understandings in congregational consciousness.[48]

The aim throughout this chapter has been to demonstrate that imaginative engagement is vital in preaching in the lyrical voice. Such preaching embraces all aspects of imaginative function. It requires that preachers exercise their sensory imagination, shaping powerful descriptive imagery to communicate aspects of the biblical text and appealing to the sensory imagination of the hearer through their use of language. The intuitive imagination fuses images and ideas together, seeking powerful metaphors and looking for the connections between material in the passage and aspects of contemporary life. Employing the affective imagination allows the preacher to stand in the shoes of the biblical characters and consider the text from the perspectives of their hearers. The intellectual imagination explores the 'if . . . then' structure of supposition. In the case of Example 1 above, *if* Jesus the storm bringer creates 'a tempest of realization that tears up our self-reliance', uprooting 'our pint-sized idols' *then* what are the implications?

Lyrical preaching is fundamentally dependent on the employment of imagination in all its functions.

---

48 Buttrick, *Homiletic Moves and Structures*, p. 191.

4

The Sacramental Potential
of Preaching

Sacraments draw our attention to the 'more' present in the everyday. They engage our imaginations, operating as windows, drawing us in to capture new vision. There is a materiality about the stuff of sacrament; the ordinary becoming translucent as we apprehend something of a greater reality mediated through the mundane. If we recognize that there is a materiality about language that has the power to disclose the 'more', then we can begin to see that there is a profound sacramentality about preaching. The sermon is a potential bearer of disclosure that can help the hearer to reframe their view of themselves, their neighbour and the world in the light of the self-revealing love of God. Seeing this disclosure, framing it, communicating it, receiving it and responding to it requires the active engagement of the imagination in all four functions. We notice and name grace through the sensory function; make connections between Scripture and the everyday in the intuitive function; feel the pain and dis-grace of the world, as well as the joy of life, in the affective function; shape ethical responses formulated around the 'if . . . then' model of the intellectual imagining. This chapter discusses the sacramental potential of preaching and its connection with the vital place of imagination in preaching.

Sacramentality: naming the 'more'

Broadly speaking we can say that a sacrament is a holy sign, which conveys grace and therefore has a vital role in building up the faithful.

By the sacramental is commonly understood the physical or material mediating that which is beyond itself, the spiritual; in the familiar definition 'the outward and visible sign of an inward and spiritual grace.'[1]

At first glance this understanding seems to exclude language from a definition of that which might be regarded as having sacramental potential since it is not material in the same sense, for example, as bread and wine. However, language springs from our very materiality. Words are learned through early bodily need. They are formed from breath, shaped by muscle movement and communicated with bodily gesture: language is profoundly material. Just as bread and wine and water form the materiality of the Eucharist, 'Words are the stuff of preaching.'[2]

If we accept, drawing on Romans 1.20, that in the economy of God's grace creation can make present to us the reality of God, and if we also accept that language is an aspect of creation and has a materiality about it, then there is every reason to explore the theological and practical implications of preaching as sacrament. This is not to argue for preaching to be recognized as a third, or eighth sacrament, but to point to the Orthodox and Catholic principle of sacramentality that sees all reality as potentially acting as bearer of God's saving presence.

Salvation is not restricted to seven channels of communication. The totality of salvation is communicated to the totality

---

1 David Brown and Ann Loades (eds), *Christ the Sacramental Word: Incarnation, Sacrament and Poetry*, London: SPCK, 1996, p. 4.

2 Donald Coggan, *A New Day for Preaching: The Sacrament of the Word*, London: SPCK, 1996, p. 17.

of human life and is manifested in a significantly tangible way in the pivotal points of life.[3]

The seven sacraments can be seen as 'nodal points', key aspects of life that condense and focus the presence of God. Embracing specific sacraments – be they two or seven – does not rule out a wider understanding of the sacramental principle and does not prevent exploration of the possibility that preaching may have a sacramental structure and function.

Sacramental theology can be seen to be underpinned by a doctrine of creation that affirms the significance of matter.

> Everything in creation, from the exploding cosmos to the whirling, dancing, utterly mysterious quantum particles, discloses something about God. And, in doing so, brings God among us.[4]

God is involved in creation and matter reveals something of the creator God. On the basis of such thinking everything has sacramental potential.[5] Creation is God's self-expression, revealing his omnipotence, omniscience and benevolence, as well as his artistry, relationality and spontaneity. In short, creation speaks something of the life of God.

However, there are some potential difficulties in basing sacramental theology on the doctrine of creation. Creation does not act as an unambiguous pointer to the divine. If it did, there would be no need for ecclesial sacraments. Creation is ambiguous – 'the mystery of evil has always been a sticking point for natural theology'.[6] In theory everything could have a

---

3 Leonardo Boff, *Sacraments of Life: Life of the Sacraments*, Washington, DC: Pastoral Press, 1987, p. 60.

4 Andrew Greeley, *The Catholic Imagination*, Berkeley and Los Angeles: University of California Press, 2000, pp. 6–7.

5 Boff, *Sacraments of Life*, p. 47. See also John Macquarrie, *A Guide to the Sacraments*, London: SCM Press, 1997, p. 8; Kenan B. Osborne, *Christian Sacraments in a Postmodern World: A Theology for the Third Millennium*, New York: Paulist Press, 1999, p. 140.

6 Macquarrie, *Guide to the Sacraments*, p. 10.

sacramental nature attributed to it, but in reality our existence is marked by both the presence of God and our separation from God. We cannot fix a place or construct and say that *this* operates sacramentally, in a final and definitive way. Neither can we exclude the potential of anything within creation speaking to us of God. Strangely, in the situations that speak only of God's absence there may still be a longing for God, a seeking of presence-in-absence. Perhaps this sacrament of absence mediates to us something of our inbuilt longing for God.

A sacrament requires both the action of God and a human response, the latter being secondary but essential. Therefore sacramental potential may not be realized because sinful humanity is closed to the possibility of God and makes no response.

Sacramentality: creation and sin

The principal danger in an appeal to the sacramentality of creation is that it underplays the fracture created by sin between revelation and creation. If creation has the inherent capacity to bear unambiguous divine meaning, why do baptism and Eucharist both imply a movement of re-creation? If creation itself is sacramental, why is there this need for such regeneration and reintegration? Rowan Williams, in exploring the logical movement of ecclesial sacraments, questions the broader principle of the sacramentality of creation. His view is that sacramental actions indicate a movement from one reality to another, into the gift of a new identity given in the rite itself.[7] This inherent sense of movement from estrangement to belonging can be opposed to any 'bland appeal to the natural sacredness of things'.[8] Is Williams right to warn us away from seeing the divine presence around us in all things?

---

7 Rowan Williams, 'Sacraments of the New Society', in *Christ the Sacramental Word*, ed. David Brown and Ann Loades, London: SPCK, 1996, pp. 89–90.

8 Williams, 'Sacraments of the New Society', p. 90.

If the connection between revelation and creation is utterly fractured by sin, bridged only by the agency of God revealed in the person of Christ, this raises the question of how the revelation of Christ to material beings operates if not through the materiality of the world. Is creation so distorted that God cannot reveal Godself through the natural world, even in a way that we might only perceive in a fragmented manner?

> Is the divine Word entirely absent from the wider world from which it singles out special elements for a specially sacred use? . . . Do they not lend themselves to such a use because God made them, because they are his creatures?[9]

What about the material nature of the revelation of God seen throughout Scripture through the natural world, through symbols and ultimately in flesh? What of the sense of the numinous experienced through nature, the love shared between humans or acts of courage and sacrifice? Do such things have nothing to do with God? If they are not signs of God, of the Other, then what are they? What of sermons that have incorporated, along with biblical material (itself the creation of human witnesses), narratives from everyday life to enable people to see God and to inspire people to seek God? How do we account for preaching that has, through material words, spoken by ordinary people, brought new perspective and ushered in a new reality into the hearers' lives? Is all of this discounted on the basis of the impossibility of God being revealed in the sinful, material world? Such an argument inflates the power of sin in relation to divine power and stresses the transcendence of God at the expense of divine immanence, peddling the heresy that God is utterly separate from the material, and yet, 'God never acts outside of men and women.'[10]

---

9 Donald M. Baillie, *The Theology of the Sacraments and Other Papers*, London: Faber & Faber, 1957, p. 43.

10 Edward Schillebeeckx, *God is New Each Moment*, Edinburgh: T. & T. Clark, 1983, p. 66.

Mary Catherine Hilkert helps here with a thesis that holds together the negative assessment of the sacramental inherent in dialectical theology with what she terms the 'sacramental imagination'.

> Dialectical theology affirms that sin has destroyed the image of God in creation, along with the human ability to discern anything of God, hence the need for Christ's redemptive action. The sacramental imagination asserts that in the face of sin, grace abounds and God can be apprehended in the human story, albeit in a fragmented way.[11]

To preach effectively we need to wrestle with the hard word that sin distorts our vision of God, our relationships and our understanding; that the Church is always in need of critique and reform; that the kingdom of God is not yet fully realized and the tragedy of the cross is the key to all reality.[12] At the same time, the sacramental imagination affirms the goodness of creation and of the human body and regards history, creation and human life, of which the Scriptures are a part, as full of revelatory potential. Sin is not negated in this view but it is relegated in its power:

> At the heart of the sacramental imagination is the conviction that in spite of all that is broken or contradictory, the power of God's grace is stronger than the power of human sin.[13]

Hilkert's sacramental imagination keeps us open to the *possibility* of finding and being found by God in creation. It keeps us open to meeting God in the material: nature and environment,

---

11 Mary Catherine Hilkert, *Naming Grace: Preaching and the Sacramental Imagination*, New York: Continuum, 1997, p. 104.

12 Hilkert, *Naming Grace*, pp. 189–90.

13 Hilkert, *Naming Grace*, p. 191.

movement and music, art and architecture and language.[14] Ann Loades reminds us to be alert to the sacramental potential of the tradition, pointing to the way the lives of the saints, including the 'almost nobodies', can mediate the divine presence to us. She gathers this sacramental resource up with many others, ranging from gardening and engineering to embroidering and food, calling for us to 'live sacramentally in our risky, mistake-ridden, very complex world'.[15] Her understanding of sacramentality is not based on a bland appeal to sacredness; rather she uses words from Rowan Williams' foreword to *The Gestures of God*, in tension with his earlier perspective, to indicate the view that sacramentality is 'the very specific conviction that the world is full of the life of God whose nature is known in Christ and the Spirit'.[16] Williams' earlier argument about the logic of the movement inherent in sacramental action, which reminds us to be hesitant about bland appeals to the sacramental principle, can thus be held in tension with the view that God, in divine creativity and grace, does speak through the banal and the ordinary aspects of the world. The graced sacramental actions and words of the Church are needed to connect humanity to the Christian narrative of salvation, set forth and becoming complete in Christ. Arguing that salvation is a process that is becoming complete in Christ is not to argue that the cross is anything other than a once-for-all act. Rather it indicates that our apprehension, reception and growth into this salvation is a process, one that works with the sacramentality of creation and requires the sacramental aspects of ecclesial life, which includes preaching.

14 See David Brown, *God and the Enchantment of Place: Reclaiming Human Experience*, Oxford: Oxford University Press, 2006; *God and Grace of Body: Sacrament in Ordinary*, Oxford: Oxford University Press, 2007; *God and Mystery in Words: Experience through Metaphor and Drama*, Oxford: Oxford University Press, 2008.

15 Ann Loades, 'Finding New Sense in the Sacramental', in *The Gestures of God*, ed. Geoffrey Rowell and Christine Hall, London: Continuum, 2004, pp. 164–5.

16 Rowan Williams, 'Preface' to *The Gestures of God*, ed. Geoffrey Rowell and Christine Hall, London: Continuum, 2004, p. xiii.

Sacramentality and incarnation

Given that in the incarnation the value of the material is stressed ('the Word became flesh and lived among us'[17]), would it be more coherent to base a sacramental theology on the incarnation rather than on creation? Loades and Brown maintain that the incarnation strengthens the connection between God and the material world. Their argument runs that in Genesis, divine transcendence is not breached by the relationship between God and the word he speaks. There is 'no intrinsic relation between God and his chosen medium',[18] whereas 'in the Johannine description of the Word made flesh, the Word has become that which binds world and God together'.[19] While Loades and Brown's argument is helpful in its conclusion, an affirmation of the sacramental nature of language, it seems questionable to conceive of the Word in creation as a mere matter of indicative speech rather than the creative act of the Triune God, which in itself forges a deep connection between God and the material. The creation itself affirms the importance of the material to the God who creates and sustains it.

The sacramental principle seems to rest most naturally on the doctrine of creation. However, we can view Christ as having a sacramental function in his humanity in that he reveals the powerful vulnerability of a God who becomes limited, who embraces being at a particular point in history, accepting the limitations of space and time. In this the incarnation acts as a sacrament of the humility of God.

Too close an identification between incarnation and the sacramental perspective can mar the singularity of the incarnation as an event in human history. God's presence with us *now* is not in flesh after the pattern of the incarnation but in Spirit illuminating

17 John 1.14.

18 David Brown and Ann Loades (eds), *The Sense of the Sacramental: Movement and Measure in Art and Music, Place and Time*, London: SPCK, 1995, p. 2.

19 Brown and Loades (eds), *Sense of the Sacramental*, p. 3.

and enlivening the material. In the Eucharist and in the sermon, Christ is revealed by the power of the Spirit but does not take on flesh. In physical terms, bread and wine remain bread and wine and human words also remain human. Preaching is not an incarnational action – Christ is not made flesh again. To argue that would be to come dangerously close to saying that the preacher in themselves incarnates Christ. Regarding creation as the basis for the sacramental perspective avoids this pitfall.

Some understandings of the real presence come close to claiming a re-enactment of both the incarnation and Christ's sacrifice. However, Donald Baillie points out that Jesus' death, resurrection and ascension all 'seem to drop into the background when we take the Church as simply the extension of the incarnation'.[20] Allied to this point is the giving of the Spirit. The Johannine material indicates an anticipated discontinuity between the time of Christ's presence in flesh and his presence in Spirit.[21] Although the physical presence of Christ will cease, Christ's presence in Spirit will continue to guide, teach, comfort and help, enabling a seeing that is beyond physical sight; a perception of deeper knowing.[22] Here we see the connection between imagination and revelation, the Spirit inviting and enabling us to see through the windows of all that God enables to function sacramentally to perceive the presence of Christ. 'Without the Spirit, sacraments are no more than sunshine on blind eyes or a voice to the deaf.'[23] Preaching becomes empty; dead words on deaf ears.

Language: painting new vistas

If words are natural phenomena that, like other elements, can open a window on to the transcendent and convey a sense of

---

20 Baillie, *Theology of the Sacraments*, p. 62.

21 John 14.26.

22 John 14.16–17, 19, 26; 15.26.

23 James F. White, *The Sacraments in Protestant Practice and Faith*, Nashville, TN: Abingdon Press, 1999, p. 20.

that transcendence to us, is there any justification for the separation between word and sacrament? If 'sound is the most fundamental category by which we can conceive God',[24] then the separation of material symbol and verbal image seems misconceived. Do words point to the reality that transcends them or actually mediate that reality to us? Are words merely indicative or does language have transformative power? Does God's revelation operate through human language? Can language function sacramentally?

Karl Barth wrestles with this question in relation to preaching. People come to church with an expectation, longing to hear the word of God spoken, and yet 'The word of God on the lips of man is an impossibility; it does not happen: no one will ever accomplish it or see it accomplished.'[25] However, surely all divine speech is mediated though human speech, for we have no other words; if the word of God is not on the lips of humanity then God is silenced and there can be no knowledge of God. Karl Rahner develops this point, arguing that God's revelation must come in one of two ways: either a theophanic vision of divine light or 'he comes in word'.[26] Rahner is clear that the utterance and perception of God's word is an act of divine grace, but one that can be known. 'The light of grace shines also by burning the oil of this world.'[27] Applying the concept of God's outpouring of himself in humility, Rahner suggests that the Word descends and inhabits all words: 'the word of God can take on the form of a slave and be found as a human word of the street'.[28] In contrast with Barth, in Rahner we see continuity between creation and redemption. In this

---

24 Stephen H. Webb, *The Divine Voice: Christian Proclamation and the Theology of Sound*, Grand Rapids, MI: Brazos Press, 2004, p. 32.

25 Karl Barth, *The Word of God and the Word of Man*, New York and Evanston: Harper & Row, 1957, p. 124.

26 Karl Rahner, 'Priest and Poet', in *Theological Investigations Vol. 3, Theology of the Spiritual Life*, London: Darton, Longman & Todd, 1967, p. 303.

27 Rahner, 'Priest and Poet', p. 313.

28 Rahner, 'Priest and Poet', p. 314.

view preaching is about speaking a word that unlocks the ability to respond to God which, by grace, is within the person already.

In discussing the power and scope of language, Rahner sets up a contrast between utility words and primordial or depth words. The former are words that convey information, indicative in purpose: these are the 'worn-down verbal coins of daily intellectual intercourse'. While God may choose to inhabit such words, it is to primordial language that Rahner looks as having the richest potential to function sacramentally. By primordial words Rahner means language that is more akin to poetry. Such language is multivalent and tensive; it 'brings the reality it signifies to us, makes it "present", realizes it and places it before us'. He also argues that anyone who has 'not sunk completely into spiritual death'[29] is capable of uttering such depth language, but he points to the poet as the one with the particular gift and calling to shape such words.

Rahner helps us to reclaim a sense of the power and sacramental potential of language. Words are part of our material existence. They imprint themselves upon our brains, with layered and complex levels of meaning and association. Words can point to a reality beyond and simultaneously communicate aspects of that reality; a love letter can both describe and evoke the presence of the lover. Talking therapies rest on the broad principle that by naming and narrating, the individual can express and experience the pain with which they wrestle. The words used to narrate the symbolic aspects of the Eucharist act referentially but are also to be taken in and chewed over as they create images of the last supper, making present imaginatively that to which they refer. The power of language is to be celebrated:

Words create new possibilities. Words preserve memories. Words change relationships and worlds. Words break hearts

---

29 Rahner, 'Priest and Poet', pp. 298, 299, 301.

and mend them. Words cause grief and give hope. Words move us to action.[30]

Words are more than signs pointing beyond themselves; words do something. J. L. Austin reminds us of the performative power of language. He identifies three dimensions of language: locutions, illocutions and perlocutions.[31] These dimensions refer to what is said, what is done by the utterance and its psychological effect.

In Austin's theory, illocutionary utterance does something. Examples include baptizing a child, naming a ship, making a bet or saying wedding vows. The perlocutionary power of language, however, lies not in what the words do but in the potential effect of such speaking; that is, in the psychological response to the words. For example, the illocutionary force of the words 'Your sins are forgiven' announces a new relationship between the hearer and God. The perlocutionary impact of these words is intended to be one of comfort, hope and peace. The performative power of such liturgical declaration can be compared with preaching the gospel, arguing that 'declaring God's persistent and relentless love for us in Jesus Christ bears the reality it asserts'.[32] Here the sacramental potential of preaching becomes clear as it seeks to awaken the hearer to the reality of God with us, eliciting an appropriate psychological response: for example, the determination to live out, or perform, the gospel in everyday life.

The imaginative preacher needs to have a care for the words they use and the work they expect words to do. Thoughtless use of language – such as non-inclusive terminology or derogatory slang – can exercise negative perlocutionary force, destroying the sacramental nature of the preaching event. The performative

---

30 Hilkert, *Naming Grace*, p. 60.

31 J. L. Austin, *How to do Things with Words*, Oxford: Clarendon Press, 1962, p. 108.

32 James R. Nieman, 'Preaching that Drives People from the Church', in *A Reader on Preaching: Making Connections*, ed. David Day, Jeff Astley and Leslie J. Francis, Aldershot: Ashgate, 2005, p. 249.

power of sermons can be negatively derailed by illustrations in which 'all women are ditzy, all men are heroes, and all the children are just props'.[33] The performative nature of preaching is a vital aspect of its sacramental nature, for which words matter profoundly.

The sacramentality of preaching

Paul Janowiak argues for 'liturgical proclamation as a sacramental act'.[34]

Boff claims that 'prophetic proclamation is a sacrament'.[35] Loades makes a similar point in arguing that sacramental understanding will 'give pride of place to preaching'.[36] Brown finds elements of understanding preaching as a sacramental act in both Catholic and Protestant thought, identifying in the theologies of both denominations encounter as a vital purpose in preaching.[37] Christoph Schwöbel speaks of the potential for the 'sanctification of human communication', the Spirit communicating God's word through our human words.[38] Edward Farley goes as far as to suggest that 'preaching may be Protestantism's primary sacrament'.[39] These points strongly support the view that preaching has sacramental potential.

This idea is strengthened by applying Boff's analysis of the threefold dimensions of a sacrament to preaching:

---

33 Nieman, 'Preaching that Drives People from the Church', p. 251.

34 Paul Janowiak, *The Holy Preaching: The Sacramentality of the Word in the Liturgical Assembly*, Collegeville, MN: Liturgical Press, 2000, p. 4.

35 Boff, *Sacraments of Life*, p. 91.

36 Loades, 'Finding New Sense in the Sacramental', p. 162.

37 Brown, *God and Mystery in Words*, pp. 112–13.

38 Christoph Schwöbel, 'The Preacher's Art: Preaching Theologically', in *Theology through Preaching*, ed. Colin E. Gunton, Edinburgh: T. & T. Clark, 2001, p. 4.

39 W. Edward Farley, 'Can Preaching Be Taught?', *Theology Today* 62:2 (2005), p. 176.

It [a sacrament] *remembers the past*, where the experience of grace and salvation burst into the world; it keeps alive the memory of the cause of all liberation, Jesus Christ and the history of his mystery. A sacrament also *celebrates a presence in the here and now of faith*: that is, grace being made visible in the rite and being communicated to human life. Thirdly, a sacrament *anticipates the future* in the present: that is eternal life, communion with God, and the shared banquet with all the just.[40]

In the Eucharist we remember God's presence in the person of Christ, we are receptive to the depth of the present moment, to the intimacy of God's presence communicated through the materiality of bread, wine and word, and we anticipate his coming again. Likewise the sermon stands as an event in time in which the community *remembers* God's work in salvation history: anamnesis is an aspect of the sermon. In the Eucharist the prayer of epiclesis seeks the blessing of the Spirit that 'these gifts of bread and wine may be to us the body and blood of our Lord Jesus Christ'. This is a prayer that the materiality of the elements will nourish and sustain us in the given moment and beyond. Similarly, a sermon that begins with a form of prayer asking that God takes and blesses the preacher's words is demonstrating the hope that the sermon will awake us to the reality of God, mediated through the materiality of fleshy language, *in the here and now*, and sustain us in the future: epiclesis is an aspect of the sermon. The Eucharist also orientates us to the future as we look for Christ's coming in glory and to eating and drinking in Christ's kingdom. Similarly, preaching has an important element of eschatological hope, anticipating the future when we are gathered up into God's new creation.

Jürgen Moltmann writes of the dual focus of 'Easter hope', which 'shines forwards into the unknown newness of the history which it opens up' as well as illuminating the 'graveyards of history', which have in their midst the 'grave of a crucified

---

40 Boff, *Sacraments of Life*, pp. 84–5; emphasis in original.

man'.[41] Moltmann's perspective is applicable to a sacramental understanding of preaching. Eschatological hope comes in the promise of God, which has the potential to transform the way we interact with present issues and also how we see the broken history of humanity needing to be transformed in new creation. This reminds the preacher that the sermon must be concerned with more than parochial issues. Because preaching is concerned with God's work in the material, sermons need to be earthed in matter and not become vacuous, bland, over-spiritualized or disengaged. Preachers need to be able to articulate hope for the past atrocities and injustices in the world. The voices of the broken and abused must be remembered and their stories articulated, just as the promise of the God of resurrection power must be named. There is more at stake here than a pep talk for living well! The ability to see God at work in the past, to discern his presence in the present moment and to anticipate his promises for the future requires the active and disciplined engagement of the imagination, whether that is in the sacrament of the Eucharist or the sacramental nature of preaching.

In the traditional understanding, sacraments combine sign and word together, shaping and mediating the event. In preaching, the word is obviously that which is spoken and which is at the same time a sign pointing beyond itself, with the potential to make present that to which it refers. There is another sign operative in the preaching event: the humanity of the preacher. The preacher's humanity is the material of a sacramental sign in the preaching event: a sign that God speaks to people through people; a sign of the centrality of relationship in Christian faith. Preachers come from the people of God to the people of God; a sign of the embodied and material nature of faith, which is utterly dependent on God, and a sign of the God who speaks into the vulnerability and specificity of the present moment. Kay Northcutt, in her hermeneutic of

---

41 Jürgen Moltmann, *The Crucified God*, London: SCM Press, 1984, p. 123.

preaching as spiritual direction (explored further in the following chapter), makes the apt point that the preacher whose deep love and desire for God is reflected in their preaching acts as a sacramental image through which we are attracted to God. This is not because of any moral superiority on the part of the preacher. Rather when the hearer recognizes the preacher's willingness to wrestle with difficult issues, to pay attention to God in the Scriptures, and the day-to-day muddle of life, authority is granted and the preacher becomes a sacramental, embodied image through which God attracts.[42]

Haecceitas comes from the Latin *haec*, meaning 'this'. There is a particular 'thisness' about any sacramental event. 'No actual baptism can ever be repeated; no actual Eucharist can ever be repeated.'[43] To this I would add, 'No actual *sermon* can ever be repeated.' There is an 'eventedness' about the sermon, the *haecceitas* of preaching, which is dependent on context, which necessarily includes participants. A sermon is among *this* group of people, with *this* preacher, in *this* particular liturgical setting, at *this* moment in time. Even a scripted sermon delivered and then repeated at another venue is not the same sermon because it is not the same event. We can draw an analogy here between preaching and musical or dramatic performances. Like such performances, each sermon is specific and vulnerable. It can claim no inherent revelatory power, but only rest on the hope that God has revealed Godself through the speaking of the preacher and the listening of the gathered before and may do so again. Recognizing the *haecceitas* of each sermon event should increase the sense of engagement and expectancy on the part of preacher and hearer.

This vision of the sacramental potential of preaching raises some considerable objections, relating to both the content and structure of sermons. How do we address the reality of evil in

---

42 Kay L. Northcutt, *Kindling Desire for God: Preaching as Spiritual Direction*, Minneapolis, MN: Fortress Press, 2009, pp. 27–9.

43 Kenan B. Osborne, *Christian Sacraments in a Postmodern World: A Theology for the Third Millennium*, New York: Paulist Press, 1999, p. 58.

the world and not mute human suffering? How do we preach presence in absence? We need to be honest that, while language has the potential to open up new vistas of hope, it can also manipulate, twist and enslave. Preaching that claims the divine imprimatur to sanction the status quo lacks any sense of imagination redeemed by God's grace and reveals nothing of God because it effects no spiritual–ethical change. The key is to note that preaching occurs in communities – communities that are called to inaugurate the kingdom through deeds as well as words, communities that bear the responsibility for naming the misuse of language and any denigration of the sermon into an anti-sacrament. In this understanding preaching is an activity and responsibility of the whole Church.

If preaching is to be received as a sacrament then it is important that it is seen as a communal calling, calling for response to God from preacher and congregation, openness, a desire to hear together and a willingness to engage. 'The human response in a sacramental event, even though secondary, is an integral part of the interrelational encounter that constitutes sacramentality.'[44] Preaching is a shared responsibility of holy speaking and holy listening. Using the Eucharist as an analogy, the use of stale bread and sour wine would affect the ability of the participant to experience the fullness of God mediated through the physicality of the elements, the elements themselves distracting from the sacrament. Equally, if the preacher uses stale words, worn-out phrases, poorly constructed images, combined with sloppy delivery, then the realization of the full sacramental possibility of preaching is likely to be severely impeded. Staying with the analogy of the Eucharist, if we receive carelessly this does not mean we haven't received but that we have missed much of the resonance and taste, like bolting a meal and not noticing flavour, texture or contrast. With the eyes of the imagination closed we will miss much of the sacramental potential of preaching. Similarly, in the preaching event the holy listening of the hearer involves chewing over the words of the sermon

---

44 Osborne, *Christian Sacraments in a Postmodern World*, p. 142.

and the biblical text, in conversation with personal and communal narratives, prayerfully and expectantly.

Is this a realistic expectation? Results from a pilot survey into preaching, although small scale (197 respondents across five denominations), suggested that 97 per cent look forward to hearing sermons either 'frequently' or 'sometimes'.[45] This sense of anticipation *may* suggest a desire on the part of congregations to experience sermons that operate sacramentally. Even allowing for the fact that those respondents were self-selecting, with people perhaps feeling they *should* report a level of anticipation to the sermon, the percentage is still remarkably high.

The nature of Anglican worship has been described as 'bi-focal', holding together the importance of Word and Sacrament.[46] Perhaps inevitably, some traditions within the Church of England seem to lay more stress on one than the other. However, if the sacramental shape and function of the sermon is recognized, then the sermon and the Eucharist are drawn more closely together. In some ways it becomes illogical to separate them into separate categories of 'Word' and 'Sacrament', as though they could be separated into neat verbal and visible units. The sermon, like the Eucharist, combines the visible and the verbal in sacramental action. As with the sermon, the words used in the Eucharist are much more than indicative in function. The language used strengthens and adds depth and resonance to the material aspect of the sacrament. For example, the words 'Take, eat, this is my body given for you' are rich with resonances of gift, sustenance, sacrifice and incorporation. Without the words the Eucharist would lack some of this depth. Language builds pictures and impressions that interact with the visual images to create layered and rich fields of meaning.

---

45 Ben Blackwell, Kate Bruce and Peter Phillips, *The View from the Pew*, Durham: CODEC, 2009, p. 8.

46 Donald Coggan, *On Preaching*, London: SPCK, 1978, p. 3.

Holding together word and visual image in preaching and the Eucharist offers a countercultural critique of the current ascendancy of the visual image. The Church is one of the few places in contemporary culture in which people gather to hear the spoken word. This is not at the expense of the visible image; the two are held together as elements of the sacramental event.

Implications for homiletic praxis

Regarding preaching as sacramental has implications for our approach to the content and construction of the sermon. The imagination operating with sacramental alertness, vital to preaching, holds to the fundamental goodness of creation; revelation is not hermetically sealed within the pages of Scripture but is to be found in people's lives. Hilkert sees 'preaching as the art of naming grace found in the depths of the human experience'.[47] If we are seeking to name grace, then the sensory function of imagination will be attentive and focused on the details of creation and of people's stories. The intuitive imagination will make connections between Scripture, theology and everyday life, looking to name God in the world. The affective function of the imagination helps the preacher to exercise and discern grace as they imagine the perspectives of the other. The intellectual imagination helps to orientate right ethical responses to seeing God in the world, using the 'if . . . then' structure of hypothesis. For example: *if* the universe is created and loved by God, *then* we have a responsibility to do what we can to care for the environment; *if* I accept the commandment to love my neighbour as myself, *then* I need to scrutinize how I treat others to ensure that my beliefs are reflected in my actions.

This presents a challenge to approaches to preaching that remain within the horizons of the biblical texts, in what might be seen as a verse-based teaching model. Preaching is more than this. Imaginative preaching will seek to connect God's word in

---

47 Hilkert, *Naming Grace*, p. 44.

the Scriptures with the life of God in the world, being honest about the difficulties inherent in working with sacred texts that are necessarily human and therefore not always obviously discernible as the word of God, and being honest that often the world seems to display an absence of God. By naming the present signs of grace in the world, preaching can point beyond to the completion of such hope in Christ. But does this take seriously the reality of evil?

One way of doing this is to reclaim the tradition of lament for preaching. The structure of lament is inherently imaginative. The lament tradition finds words to bear and expresses the distress of the community or individual. Lament then recounts the faithfulness of God and reorientates the faithful on the basis of trust in God. The future hope is never realized within the lament itself, so in that sense lament is always open-ended. Similarly, sacramental preaching can never be too neatly closed. 'The temptation for the Christian preacher is to "offer solutions" rather than to attend to the anguish of the assembly and to entrust the pain to God'.[48] Whether it names grace or disgrace, the sermon is always pointing beyond itself. By nature, preaching seeks to open the Church to deeper engagement with God in prayer and action. On that basis, sermons must not be too finished or too neatly completed. The aim of a sermon is to have a life beyond the time-bound period of its utterance. This has structural implications for the sermon. There are many possible ways of keeping the sermon focused outward, such as a structure that weaves questions of application throughout or one that builds towards a sermonic ending that opens outward. Not every sermonic question should be or can be answered.

To bring to speech the deepest experiences of human being requires a contemplative aspect to the preacher's life. Hilkert argues that preachers need to be in touch with their own deepest struggles in order to be attuned to the issues of dis-grace in the world. Effectively, she is arguing that preaching be recognized as a spiritual discipline, embracing prayer and imagination.

---

48 Hilkert, *Naming Grace*, p. 116.

Imagination, with the 'power to reconfigure reality by seeing it through an alternative lens',[49] is central to sacramental preaching. It takes imaginative insight to make connections between the depth experiences of doubt, fear and confusion and the hope of the gospel and imaginative vision to discern the grace at work in the suffering of the world. Inherent to preaching is the prophetic ability to make connections between God's past faithfulness, his continuing fidelity and the promise of hope. Making these connections calls for an imaginative openness to the Spirit. The dynamic of imaginative contemplation and action has the potential to shape sermons that are honest and realistic in their naming of grace and dis-grace and able also to move beyond naming into shaping active response, in penitence or praise, or political and ethical action.

If we accept that language can function sacramentally, then the words of the sermon matter. Not that linguistic and performative skill alone can reveal God but that God can use the giftedness of imagination, language use and performance to break open the scriptural word and point to the reality of the incarnate Word, who by grace breathes through the event of the sermon. Language that names the depths of human experience or seeks to enable the congregation to soar in hope and worship belongs to the palette of the poet. Such language is 'shattering, evocative speech that breaks fixed conclusions and presses us always toward new, dangerous and imaginative possibilities'.[50] Preaching that seeks to learn from poetry is preaching that seeks to articulate depth experience, to subvert, to surprise, to provoke and to delight. It is incumbent on the preacher to wrestle with language and find imagery that will enable a new seeing.

The words a preacher utters spring from the physicality of the person in terms of pitch, volume, facial expression and bodily

49 Hilkert, *Naming Grace*, p. 188.

50 Walter Brueggemann, *Finally Comes the Poet: Daring Speech for Proclamation*, Minneapolis, MN: Fortress Press, 1989, p. 6.

gesture. 'We speak with our limbs as well as our throats'.[51] Accepting that preaching operates sacramentally, by God's grace opening up the possibilities of seeing and experiencing the divine, then preachers naturally have a calling to develop their skills in performance. Performance is perhaps a controversial word, implying something artificial, an acted-out pretence. However, if we take the word 'performance' as meaning to make present before the other that which has been internalized, there is no danger of a lack of integrity. Richard Ward argues that the term 'performance' is to be preferred to 'delivery' since the latter term implies that preaching is merely a transaction in which the preacher 'delivers' theological goods:

> 'Performance' is a richer, more integrative schema for putting the elements of language, action, and form, together with speech, gesture, and embodiment in the event of preaching.[52]

A performance requires the involvement of the hearer for it to have meaning; it speaks of a communal event.

This chapter has sought to analyse the sacramental potential of preaching, based on a theology of creation, which underscores the revelatory power of language in the preaching event. It reminds us of the shared task of preaching; ecclesial sacraments being communal actions of the Church. Like the visual image, language too has a multivalent, tensive potential. Recognizing this strengthens the connection between word and sacrament. Grasping the sacramentality of preaching has implications for understanding the nature and praxis of preaching. It significantly strengthens the argument for preaching in the lyrical voice.

---

51 Stephen H. Webb, *The Divine Voice: Christian Proclamation and the Theology of Sound*, Grand Rapids, MI: Brazos Press, 2004, p. 58.

52 Richard F. Ward, 'Preaching as a Communicative Act: The Birth of a Performance', *Reformed Liturgy and Music* 30:2 (1996), www.religion-online.org/showarticle.asp?title=341.

5

Imagining the Preaching Task

Just who do you think you are as a preacher? The question is a serious one. How the preacher imagines, sees or looks upon their role will affect the way they engage with the task of preaching. The metaphors that master us shape our practice. This chapter evaluates six metaphors for the preacher – teacher, spiritual director, herald, artist, jazz musician, jester – and examines the implications of each. The drive of the argument is not to claim that any *one* master metaphor *should* be adopted as the best. The contention here is that the preacher needs to evaluate how they imagine their role as preacher, because these internalized models carry theological freight and will have practical out-working. Connected with this, it is important that hearers are encouraged to explore the on-looks they bring to the preaching event, which will affect the way they engage with it. Preachers can affect hearers' on-looks – for good or ill – by their attitude and pulpit demeanour. They need to employ imagination to explore the messages being communicated by their choice of words, paralinguistic 'speech' and the consequences of their underlying master metaphor(s) for the preaching act.

The preacher as teacher

What is the point of preaching? In the earliest homiletics textbook,[1] Augustine reiterates Cicero's goals of oratory:

---

1 Augustine, *De Doctrina Christiana*, Bk IV (AD 426), www.georgetown.edu/faculty/jod/augustine/ddc4.html.

'an eloquent man must speak so as to teach, to delight, and to persuade'.[2] To this end he urges that the laws of rhetoric should not be neglected – the Christian teacher must excel in eloquence. He argues that since the faculty of eloquence is available to all, 'Why do not good men study to engage it on the side of truth, when bad men use it to obtain the triumph of wicked and worthless causes, and to further injustice and error?'[3] At first glance it does seem that Augustine places all the responsibility for teaching persuasively on the preacher's skill. However, he does stress the divine agency at the heart of preaching, urging preachers to pray for themselves and their hearers before they attempt to speak – prayerful piety being more important than gifts of oratory.[4] Referring to the reception of the sermon, Augustine comments that 'no one learns aright the things that pertain to life with God, until God makes him ready to learn from himself'.[5] He again stresses the importance of the preacher's prayer, that God 'put into his mouth a suitable discourse'.[6] Augustine's model roots the initiative for the revelatory act with God but this in no way negates the skill of the preacher, who works under the agency of the Spirit.

Augustine's model of preacher as teacher is useful in that it calls on the preacher to use the artefacts of culture (in his context classical rhetoric) to help teach the Scriptures. It calls for dependency on God's grace and a responsible development and exercise of communication skills with the end goal of persuading the hearer. He comments that there is no profit in confessing truth and praising eloquence if the hearer 'does not yield his consent'. In his analysis, rhetoric is an important tool to use to this end; it has a role to play in helping to make clear what was obscure. He draws an analogy between the use of persuasive devices and adding flavour to food: 'the very food without

---

2 Augustine, *De Doctrina Christiana*, Bk IV, Ch. 12. 27.
3 Augustine, *De Doctrina Christiana*, Bk IV, Ch. 2. 3.
4 Augustine, *De Doctrina Christiana*, Bk IV, Ch. 15.
5 Augustine, *De Doctrina Christiana*, Bk IV, Ch. 16. 33.
6 Augustine, *De Doctrina Christiana*, Bk IV, Introduction; Ch. 15. 32; Ch. 16. 33; Ch. 30. 63.

which it is impossible to live must be flavoured to meet the tastes of the majority'.[7] Judging what the tastes of the majority are – never mind a consideration of the needs of the minority – requires imaginative engagement with the context, community and individual. 'Flavouring' the sermon appropriately, so that the needs of the learners are central to the educative act, requires at least the engagement of the affective function and a strong sensory imagination that notices what is going on in the hearers' environment and pays attention to the ordinary theology therein.

The effect of the Enlightenment on this model

However, Augustine's model of preacher as teacher has been reshaped by the modern emphasis on rationality and individualism.[8] The tension between divine and human agency shifted with the modernist stress on reason as the arbiter of truth. The ascendancy of Enlightenment rationalism meant that reason became the authoritative compass in society. The task of the preacher in modernity is to fit the scriptural revelation to this scientific worldview, resulting in sermons dealing with propositions extracted from Scripture, with appeals to reason and logic. David Buttrick comments:

> It is no accident that a rational, objective homiletic arose at the same time as scientific method. Rational homiletics does seem to parody scientific procedure in which an object is isolated for study and a general deduction is followed by descriptive statements.[9]

---

7 Augustine, *De Doctrina Christiana*, Bk IV, Ch. 13. 29; Ch. 11. 26.

8 David Johnson Trygve, *The Preacher as Artist: Metaphor, Identity, and the Vicarious Humanity of Christ*, PhD Thesis, University of St Andrews, 2010, http://research-repository.st-andrews.ac.uk/handle/10023/944, pp. 81–100.

9 David Buttrick, 'Interpretation and Preaching', *Interpretation* 35:1 (1981), p. 47.

The on-look of preacher as teacher, affected by the modernist turn to the self, has a number of serious negative consequences relating to:

- the handling of the biblical text;
- the shape of the sermonic form;
- the interpretation and use of figurative language;
- the relationship between faith and reason;
- the danger of adopting contemporary communication techniques as though they were neutral;
- the unhelpful stress on the distance between the pulpit and the pew.

In terms of handling the biblical text, Buttrick sees a 'method of distillation' at work when passages are reduced to single propositional 'truths'.[10] This approach implicitly places the reason of the interpreter over and against the imaginative vision of the biblical writer, and the preacher risks mutilating the particular biblical genre in extracting propositions.

The form of the subsequent sermon, rather than being shaped by the intent of the text, generally follows a deductive, logical, step-by-step, pointed shape that betrays its captivity to the end point of rational persuasion. There is no reason to dismiss the pointed deductive sermon out of hand, but it is important that the preacher is critically aware of the sermonic style they are using, the reasons for that choice, and that they are not blind to the assumptions embedded in the particular approach adopted.

The danger in the modernist understanding of the preacher as teacher can play out in the way figurative language is interpreted and deployed. The tensive, multivalent nature of such scriptural language is distorted if it is boiled down into propositions. The modernist teacher–preacher model tends to regard figurative language as ornamentation in service of the communication of rational points. However, figurative language is an essential aspect of much of the biblical material. It cannot be

---

10 Buttrick, 'Interpretation and Preaching', p. 48.

thrown aside like wrapping. Such language is restive and lively, refusing to be pinned down on a board like a butterfly, beautiful but dead.

Another potentially negative entailment of this model is the uncritical adoption of communication aids. Augustine assumed rhetoric was neutral. However, like any communication medium, rhetoric is value-laden. Can the gospel be corralled into linear logical forms? What does that do to mystery? The deductive sermon, which moves from a general statement at the outset followed by propositional proofs and application, presupposes that all can be rationally explained. Even the inductive sermon, in the teaching mode, which journeys from a specific human issue or question, tends to assume that everyone will neatly arrive at the conclusion the preacher reached in their study of the text. This seems to force a sense of uniformity on the hearers.

More recent technological communication developments carry risks if used as though they were neutral 'tools'. Use of multimedia projection packages can give support to the sermon and provide helpful material for visual learners. However, uncritical usage can have a number of deleterious effects: images carry with them their own narrative freight, which can easily tear away from the particular narrative drive of the sermon. The theological entailments of a film clip may be at odds with the theological focus of the sermon; preachers need to take care to exegete the film carefully. Images operate as 'eye candy',[11] and as long as an image is on a screen people will look to the image rather than the preacher. Judicious use of blank screens is essential to avoid seriously distorting the theological nature of the sermon as embodied event. Too many words on a screen and 'busy' slide transitions distract and relocate the focus from the interaction between hearer and preacher

---

11 Geoffrey Stevenson, 'Communication and Communion', in *Preaching with Humanity: A Practical Guide for Today's Church*, ed. Geoffrey Stevenson and Stephen Wright, London: Church House Publishing, 2008, p. 105.

to a dubious, and often irritated, interaction between viewer and screen. Using data projection to communicate the main headings of an address can result in the emphasis being shifted 'from the intention of the sermon to its information content'.[12] Adoption of new technologies such as Twitter can provide brilliant interactive opportunities when used with a filter, such as a third party monitoring a Twitter feed, passing comments or questions to the preacher at appropriate moments built into the sermon structure. Projecting tweets straight to a 'twitter fall' (a screen displaying all tweets in real time), visible to all, will tend to distract from the preacher – the eye-candy factor at work. Another risk of using Twitter in sermons is that it shuts out those who do not have access to a smartphone. However, Twitter is a very effective tool in broadcasting aspects of the sermon to a wider audience, and it enables a preacher to see how different people have heard the sermon, through an analysis of what they considered worth passing on in 140 characters.

The above list's final limitation of the preacher as teacher metaphor, in the Enlightenment model, relates to the distance and power imbalance it creates between the pulpit and the pew. There is a deeply patriarchal bias in this model, which assumes the set-apartness of the preacher. Christine Smith argues that women gain their sense of self through sustaining affiliations and relationships, through intimacy and interconnectedness. Shaped by the experience of being mothered by women, female identity tends to emphasize attachment, identification and bonding, whereas male identity is associated with differentiation and detachment from the mother. 'A boy's masculinity depends on *detachment*, a girl's femininity on her *attachment*'. On the basis of this, Smith comments that 'When the preacher is a woman, perhaps there is a radically different relational understanding at work in the act of proclamation.' There is a corrective to the masculine bias of the Enlightenment

---

12 David Heywood, *Transforming Preaching: The Sermon as a Channel for God's Word*, London: SPCK, 2013, p. 24.

preacher as teacher model in Smith's metaphor of preacher as weaver. The weaving image overcomes the distance between pulpit and pew, highlighting the essential connection between the single threads and the whole cloth. The metaphor also suggests the imaginative vision involved in preaching and the importance of design.[13]

In a 1986 address to successful female graduates at Bryn Mawr College, Pennsylvania, Ursula Le Guin differentiates between mother and father tongue.[14] The former we learn as children, 'a language always on the verge of silence and often on the verge of song'. It is the everyday language of story, subjective, conversational, common speech, which seeks to connect with others. In contrast, the father tongue is learned in the academy. It is the language of public discourse and speechmaking. Given that the father tongue is distancing, one-way communication, spoken from above, it seems this is the dialect of the Enlightenment pulpit. Le Guin praises the father tongue in its search for objectivity and yet on balance her argument 'feels' at odds with this praise. She speaks of how men have often learned that the mother tongue, with its inherent vulnerability, is not a safe language, and they forget the language of their childhood. Le Guin refers to the way that 'institutions of patriarchy' teach us to attend to those who speak the father tongue, and in so doing we can easily tune out the mother-tongue speakers.

While users of mother and father tongue may be male or female, Jeff Astley connects ordinary theology with the mother tongue and notes that more women tend to speak it than men. He observes that male God-talk tends to be more cool, analytic and detached than female, though not as detached

---

13 Christine M. Smith, *Weaving the Sermon: Preaching in a Feminist Perspective*, Louisville, KY: John Knox Press, 1989, pp. 15–21, 32–40.

14 Ursula K. Le Guin, 'Bryn Mawr Commencement Address', in *Dancing at the Edge of the World: Thoughts on Words, Women, Places*, New York: Grove Press, 1989, pp. 147–60.

as the language of the academy.[15] If ordinary theology tends towards the mother tongue, and this register focuses on relationship and trust, then perhaps preaching should attend primarily, though not exclusively, to the cadences of this speech mode.

Le Guin speaks of a third language, her 'native tongue'. This is the language of art. It is the welding of public language to private experience, the wedding of father and mother tongue. This description sounds like lyrical preaching (see Chapter 3) at its best. Artistic, tensive, bold, honest, seeking connection with the other, this is public language that notices and names the essential things of life: God; love; humanity; forgiveness; the truth of God's kingdom among us; the news of God's Spirit who summons forth our best and names and transforms our worst. This is a language that learns its cadences from the ordinary world of laughter, joy, pain, loneliness and misery, and names these realities boldly in the contexts where the father tongue, distancing, analytic, uninvolved, has often held sway.

A corrective to the flaws of the Enlightenment model

The preacher as teacher model *can* imply that the one in the pulpit is the expert, holding all the knowledge, and that the purpose of the sermon is the dissemination of that information. However, this criticism depends on a particular understanding of the role of a teacher. Teaching involves the communication of knowledge, instruction, guidance, modelling good learning, and central to all of this is the formation of the learner. If we focus on the formational role of the teacher, this helps to correct the

---

15 Jeff Astley, *Ordinary Theology: Looking, Listening and Learning in Theology*, Aldershot: Ashgate, 2002, pp. 78–80; Jeff Astley, 'Giving Voice to the Ordinary', in *Exchanges of Grace: Essays in Honour of Ann Loades*, ed. Natalie K. Watson and Stephen Burns, London: SCM Press, 2008, pp. 204–7; Anthony Lees-Smith, 'Ordinary Theology as "Mother Tongue"', in *Exploring Ordinary Theology: Everyday Christian Believing and the Church*, ed. Jeff Astley and Leslie Francis, Farnham: Ashgate, 2013, pp. 23–31.

top-down pedagogic model of the preacher as teacher. Such a teacher will begin with the hearer, will listen to their 'ordinary theology' in the dialect of the mother tongue, seeking to work with the community in discerning what God is doing in the present moment. This understanding of the preacher is perhaps better envisaged under the model of the preacher as spiritual director (a type of teacher), which is explored below.

The preacher as spiritual director

Kay Northcutt sees preaching in terms of spiritual direction. Her thesis is that:

> Preachers become as spiritual directors to their congregations, that preaching itself be a formational, sacramental act of spiritual direction, and that sermons do for congregations what spiritual direction does for individuals.[16]

There is potential for misunderstanding the nature of the authority implicit in the word 'direction'. Not to discount a director's training and expertise, their authority is not primarily conferred by the position they hold but is based upon the trust the directee places in them: a trust that grows as the relationship develops and the directee sees that the director is a person of prayer and humanity. The authority of the preacher as spiritual director is an authority based on the authenticity of their intimacy with God, rather than as an entailment of their role. This is 'sapiential authority',[17] the trust that comes through the recognition of the wisdom of the director. There is a human hunger for authenticity and trustworthiness, for welcome of the other as they are, with understanding and compassion, willing

---

16 Kay L. Northcutt, *Kindling Desire for God: Preaching as Spiritual Direction*, Minneapolis, MN: Fortress Press, 2009, p. 2.
17 John Westerhoff, *Spiritual Life: The Foundation for Preaching and Teaching*, Louisville, KY: Westminster John Knox Press, 1994, p. 49.

to offer insight and guidance. 'Formation by attraction'[18] is a vital element in learning. Preachers can act as sacramental images of attraction, their own desire for God, love of God and time spent with God becoming tangible in the preached event. This calls for preachers to ensure that prayer has priority over method in their homiletic.

In the one-to-one process of spiritual direction the director's task is to listen and discern, to apply the perceptive and imaginative eyes of faith to the directee's life in order to enable them to notice and co-operate with the movement of God. Such direction is not about problem-solving, explanation, persuasion or dispensing advice. It is a process of seeking God's shalom, God's wholeness in the lives of individuals. It assumes that God is already present in the longings and struggles of the directee. There is resonance here with Craig Dykstra's work on the pastoral and ecclesial imagination. His concept of the growth of pastoral imagination is similar to the goal of the work of the spiritual director. This involves 'seeing in depth' and 'perceiving the more' of what is before us. Like spiritual direction, exercising pastoral imagination involves 'enabling, helping, guiding and encouraging a specific community to practice Christian faith themselves'. Preaching is part of the service of that end goal. Dykstra sees pastoral imagination as a gift of God given to ministers through the ecclesial imagination of the community, which has in turn been shaped by the pastoral imagination of its ministers.[19] There is a virtuous cycle at work here that many spiritual directors would identify in their one-to-one work. The wisdom of the director comes to the fore in the relationship with the other, whose insights and growth feed back and shape the work of the director.

---

18 Margaret Miles, *Image as Insight*, Boston, MA: Beacon Press, 1961, p. 145; Northcutt, *Kindling Desire for God*, pp. 9–34.

19 Craig Dykstra, 'Pastoral and Ecclesial Imagination', in *The Life Abundant: Practical Theology, Theological Education, and Christian Ministry*, ed. Dorothy C. Bass and Craig Dykstra, Grand Rapids, MI: Eerdmans, 2008, pp. 48, 58, 59.

Preaching as spiritual direction sees loneliness, anxiety, pain and temptation as part of what it means to be human. These are not sufferings to be muted, but entered into in the deep love of God. Much human suffering cannot be solved, yet the spiritual experience of desolation can be formative as well as, at times, simply bewildering and distressing. This allows scope for the sermon as lament, even for imprecatory expression from the pulpit, on behalf of the beaten and abused, as well as for expressions of hope, trust and new possibility. This frees the preacher, and the hearer, from the pressure to pretend to be more or less than they are, hiding in fear behind a veil of false holiness and piety or playing down giftedness with false modesty. Such dishonesty can lead to a split between the private and public self, resulting in potential breakdown. The preacher needs to attend closely and honestly to their own spiritual formation. The process of their learning, including their failing and suffering, becomes a resource for their preaching – not in an unhelpfully disclosive public way but as a deep resource, a source of empathetic imaginative identification with the struggles of the other. Self-knowledge brings spiritual freedom, an ability to laugh at oneself, and – especially important for egotistical preachers! – a wry understanding of the hunger for admiration and accolade. Through their understanding of and compassion for the false self, the preacher will communicate compassion and understanding to the hearer, as a fellow-pilgrim on the way. Together we seek God, not with the preacher above or over against the congregation. The co-pilgrim preacher listens to the questions being asked and creates space for the ongoing conversation, open to being shaped by the other and willing to offer their own life as a resource for the learning of the congregation. Prayer, rather than technique, is at the heart of this model. In this model the congregation is seen as *paideuterion*, a school for wisdom,[20] in which attentiveness is cultivated and the importance of simply waiting is stressed.

---

20 Northcutt, *Kindling Desire for God*, pp. 3–5.

One of the main problems with Northcutt's thesis is that the sermon examples she gives are taken from special occasions at which she was the visiting speaker. She does not provide examples of how the preacher as spiritual director might operate week in and week out in the local church community. Her guidelines on sermon preparation portray the preacher working in isolation. She describes the preacher reflecting on what *they* have seen or felt of God at work in the congregation. However, at no point does Northcutt suggest actually talking with people about *their* concerns, about where *they* have discovered God or about *their* reflections on the Scriptures. This seems a significant oversight in an otherwise helpful model of preaching.

John McClure's model of collaborative preaching sits well with Astley's stress on listening to the ordinary theology of churchgoers. McClure comments:

> We must seek out the unique, strange and sometimes bizarre interpretations of the Gospel that are around us in our culture, in the minds and hearts of good Church people, and latent within the recesses of our own lives.[21]

In other words, we need to listen to the ordinary theology in our hearers and in ourselves. McClure identifies the importance of face-to-face symmetry between speaker and hearer in the preaching event. Inductive models, while going some way towards mitigating this asymmetry, can misconceive just how different people's experiences can be. While the affective imagination can help us to appreciate something of the experience of others, greater collaboration between preacher and hearer opens the preacher to learning from the other, respecting their very different experiences and avoiding the danger of collapsing them all into an extension of the preacher's worldview.

---

21 John S. McClure, *The Roundtable Pulpit: Where Leadership and Preaching Meet*, Nashville, TN: Abingdon Press, 1995, p. 17.

McClure's model of roundtable preaching stresses the importance of listening and shows us a practical way that preaching as spiritual direction might work in practice, though he speaks in terms of collaborative leadership rather than spiritual direction. The roundtable sermon group constitutes a cross-section of the community, rotated on a regular basis, including people on the margins as well as those more central to the community. It meets on a weekly basis to review the previous sermon and to discuss the Scriptures on which the subsequent sermon is to be based. This might raise the objection, 'Who has time for this?' However, if people are invited to attend on a short-term basis or to come along once a month, this may increase take-up. Interestingly, McClure advocates the inclusion of those who are not Christian but are associated with the Church in some way, such is his concern to connect the redemptive work of Christ to the public realm, avoiding the privatization of religion. In many ways the role McClure ascribes to the preacher in the roundtable sermon group is resonant with the role of a spiritual director. The preacher works with a co-host who manages the discussion process, freeing the preacher to listen reflectively and, where helpful, to participate. McClure offers detailed and useful guidance on managing the discussion process[22] and stresses the importance of the preacher taking time to reflect on the group process as soon as possible afterwards. It is of central importance that the process of the conversation itself finds its way into the pulpit. This model is much more collaborative than Northcutt's model of the preacher making the journey alone in their study. The preacher has the task of shaping the sermon, drawing from the process and wisdom of the group and acknowledging the difficulties people might have with the text and its implications. In McClure's worked example, the group process is often referenced in the subsequent sermon, although appropriate confidentiality is maintained.[23]

---

22 McClure, *The Roundtable Pulpit*, pp. 58–72.
23 McClure, *The Roundtable Pulpit*, pp. 95–108.

A technique often used to bring the spiritual direction meeting to a close is to ask the directee to sum up what has been significant in the meeting. Such deliberate summation helps to fix the key material in mind for further reflection and prayer. The preaching as spiritual direction model reminds the preacher to create space for reflection immediately after the sermon, so that vital themes the hearer has woven around the preached sermon are not lost. With this in mind it is important for congregations to have the opportunity to reflect on the place of the sermon in their ongoing spiritual lives as individuals and as a community. How often are congregations encouraged to reflect on the importance of active engagement with God in the event of the sermon, and after the event, as they continue to explore the particular themes they heard? When is there opportunity for congregations to reflect together concerning what they have heard in a sermon as they discern together the movement of God in their corporate life?

The on-look of the preacher as spiritual director has real potential. It places the preacher with, not above, the people, as a fellow pilgrim. It stresses the importance of seeing God at work in the ordinary, a task of imaginative perception. It notices the sacramental potential of the preacher and, if we take McClure's thesis seriously, of every member of the community. At the roundtable we may find people at the stage of 'belief that' – a third-person experience of learning about religion – alongside people who inhabit 'belief in', who embrace the faith with personal commitment, many of whom will want to 'move on' in a process of continued, inhabited learning.[24] All of them have contributions to make to the direction and life of the community as a whole. This model stresses the importance of listening, in a culture of face-to-face engagement, to give space for discovering more of the congregation's ordinary theology. The sermon seeks to find and articulate, through engagement with Scripture and congregation, what God is about among

---

24 See Astley, *Ordinary Theology*, pp. 25–34.

a community and where God is leading. The model is richly relational, based on mutual trust and prayer.

The preacher as herald

Karl Barth's homiletic draws heavily on the model of preacher as *keryx* or herald. In Barth's analysis we can never know God on the basis of our ability to translate biblical themes into rational, scientific, historical data. On the contrary, for Barth, revelation comes to us as a message from a king, through his herald, to his people.[25]

Underpinning Barth's understanding of the preacher as herald is his insistence on the sovereignty of God: 'The fixed point from which all preaching starts is the fact that God has revealed himself'.[26] The Bible is not the Word of God in the sense of a fixed, codified manual. Rather it becomes the Word of God through the interpretive agency of the Holy Spirit. Barth always privileges the biblical text above other authorities – for him this is the primary source of God's speech to us. The Scriptures are not simply texts pointing to what people believed in another age and recording God's engagement with them, rather Scripture speaks into the particularity of the present moment. The preacher's receptivity to God's word and the congregation's response are dependent upon a gift bestowed – a fresh revelatory 'event' that is preaching graced by God. The fact that a herald has anything to say depends entirely on the words they are given. Positively, the preacher as herald metaphor offers us a reminder of the sovereign grace of God, points up the preacher's dependence on God and on the Scriptures and positions prayer at the centre of the practice of preaching.

The listening of the herald is thus prior to the herald's speaking. Essential disciplines for the preacher are the disciplines of

---

25 Karl Barth, *Church Dogmatics* I/1, Edinburgh: T. & T. Clark, 1975, p. 57.

26 Karl Barth, *Prayer and Preaching*, London: SCM Press, 1964, p. 70.

hearing – prayerful, attentive, focused, obedient and courage-ous receptivity – rather than the disciplines of delivery and address.[27]

If we accept the theological assertion that preaching begins with God, there is great comfort here for the preacher who is not left alone in the study wrestling to find a word but is guided by the Living Word who interprets the Written Word and shapes the Spoken Word. This model is a corrective to the risk inherent in the other models, which can overempha-size the skill of the preacher. However, there are a number of difficulties with the preacher as herald metaphor, concern-ing the nature of revelation, the humanity of the preacher, the reduced significance of context and a flattened homiletic style.

In seeking to guard the sovereignty of God in the revelatory act, Barth runs the danger that the episodic, unpredictable nature of revelation makes God seem like the Scarlet Pimpernel – here then gone, fleeting and unreliable. In contrast to this under-standing of revelation is Bonhoeffer's assertion that:

> Our God . . . is the God who has, in the Incarnation, freely bound himself to the world. We can therefore intelligently speak about the continuity and reliability of God's revela-tion, not simply its eventfulness.[28]

A theology of preaching needs to hold together the reliability of God's self-revelation (Bonhoeffer) with the sovereignty of God's control over that revelation (Barth), if the preacher is to remain confident in God and avoid justifying their sermons on the basis of their own rhetorical efforts.

Another difficulty with Barth's homiletic is the sense that the humanity of the herald is downplayed. Barth seems to treat

---

27 William Willimon, *Conversations with Barth on Preaching*, Nashville, TN: Abingdon Press, 2006, p. 168.

28 Bonhoeffer, in Willimon, *Conversations with Barth on Preaching*, p. 173.

the preacher as a mere conduit, which implies that the listeners are little more than receptacles. If the task of the preacher is simply to pass on a message, then the task is simply one of repetition. In emphasizing the sovereignty of God, the role of the preacher is almost eclipsed. In the preacher as herald on-look there is no place for rhetorical skill; imagination is unnecessary, even dangerous, as it might confuse the message. However, in *Homiletics* Barth specifically attempts to define preaching using two formulas, which need to be held together as a way of expressing the relationship between the Word of God and the human word. These formulas are represented in a diagrammatic form here as a way of highlighting the directional thrust of both:

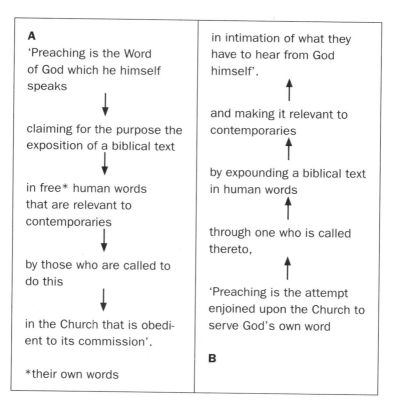

A

'Preaching is the Word of God which he himself speaks

↓

claiming for the purpose the exposition of a biblical text

↓

in free* human words that are relevant to contemporaries

↓

by those who are called to do this

↓

in the Church that is obedient to its commission'.

*their own words

in intimation of what they have to hear from God himself'.

↑

and making it relevant to contemporaries

↑

by expounding a biblical text in human words

↑

through one who is called thereto,

↑

'Preaching is the attempt enjoined upon the Church to serve God's own word

B

The preacher is not driven from sight in the Barthian homiletic task; rather (see B above, reading up the page), they are called in and with the Church to 'serve God's own word'. They are called as specific people to be themselves. Barth stresses simplicity of speech to communicate the fruit of exegesis and meditation. There is a tension here: if preachers are to be themselves they need to use their specific gifts. The fruits of imaginative labour – rhetorical skill, poetic insight, drama and humour – can be effective ways of communicating the reality of divine revelation. Lest we fall again into an over-reliance on human agency, Barth reminds us that the task of preaching is God's initiative (see A above). The fact of divine initiative does not mean, however, that the preacher can be careless about sermon construction. Barth makes the salutary comment that 'if it is true in general that we must give an account of every idle word, we must do so especially in our preaching'.[29]

The preacher as herald model seems to overlook the preacher's relationship to the congregation as a significant factor in the preaching event. Inevitably, the character of the preacher and the way the congregation receives them is a part of the event of the sermon, a point seriously downplayed in the preacher as herald model.

Barth's stress on the centrality of the biblical text tends to lead him to downplay context:

> On special occasions, e.g., the outbreak of war, the text must always stand above the theme of the day. Thoughts about the war must not be intruded into the text. More than ever in precisely these situations we must maintain obedience to the text. The Church can execute its true task only if it is not caught up in the general excitement but tries to achieve mastery over it by proclaiming what is above all things human.[30]

---

29 Karl Barth, *Homiletics*, Louisville, KY: Westminster John Knox Press, 1991, p. 119.

30 Barth, in Willimon, *Conversations with Barth on Preaching*, p. 28.

However, he contends that 'there must also be openness to the real situation of the congregation and reflection upon it so as to be able to take it up into the sermon'.[31] There seems to be contradiction here: how can the preacher be open 'to the real situation of the congregation' and not attend to the wider context that congregation lives in? To ring-fence the biblical text, not allowing it to speak into the context of the upheavals and the joys of life, seems to consign the text into a kind of holy-otherness which, if pushed too far, feels and looks rather like irrelevance. This conclusion is bolstered by Barth's warning against preachers bringing in 'social and ethical' problems to the pulpit. He argues that these issues 'will always be there to seduce a preacher into having a shot at them'.[32] Was Martin Luther King having 'a shot' at the evils of segregation? Should there have been no preaching against slavery, apartheid or segregation? Barth's stress on the biblical text does lead him to downplay the importance of context in the preaching event. Preaching must be rooted in the biblical text, seeking to do in the sermon what the text itself is doing, but this does not mean that it should be silent on social, political, economic or ethical issues. Jesus the Living Word addressed these areas in his teaching; the Written Word of Scripture addresses these areas, especially in the Prophets and the Gospels. Therefore it should come as no surprise that the Word of God in the sermon, the Spoken Word, will address such areas of human life.

Another weakness in the preacher as herald image is that it 'cashes out' in a particular homiletic style. 'Barth's sermons assert and announce, but they almost never seduce, entice, cajole, and sneak up upon the hearer'.[33] Given the artistry of the biblical texts, we should expect all the tools of rhetoric to be available to the preacher, not as mere sermonic ornamentation but as part of the preacher's artistic palette to be used in

---

31 Barth, *Homiletics*, p. 84.
32 Barth, *Homiletics*, p. 118.
33 Willimon, *Conversations with Barth on Preaching*, p. 190.

ways congruent with the theological content and communication of the message.

The homiletic tendency in more recent years has been to focus primarily on the listener, advancing methods of fostering congregational hearing. Barth would resist attempts to evoke an experience in the hearers, since that is the remit of God alone. God is the source of all our questions and the generative heart of all our experiences of preaching and listening to sermons. Undoubtedly, though, the preacher does have agency and therefore responsibility – but neither are sovereign. Humanity cannot seek through its own means to possess, control, fix or ensure the revelation of God. Any attempt to do so is idolatrous in intention, negating the lead role of God in the divine–human encounter, and failing to trust that 'we really do have a God who redeems our speech, who breathes, discloses, and declares in a way that is beyond all of our rhetoric'.[34] Nevertheless, preachers are bound to use the gifts they have, applying imagination and intelligence to ensure that the sermon is the best they can give; that in itself is an act of worship.

Barth stresses the otherness of God but seems less concerned with the earthed realities of how people hear and how preachers might helpfully communicate. He insists that preaching that 'is faithful to the Bible cannot be tedious', and urges the preacher to have the congregation constantly present in mind through the preparation of the sermon.[35] As we have seen, in avoiding tedium and speaking into the context, the preacher needs to exercise imaginative insight. However, Barth offers little by way of guidance on the shaping of the sermon. In a very short section of *Homiletics*, he argues for the sermon to be written out in full, stating that 'writing is a creative production'. He calls for orderly language, appropriate to content, on the basis that the 'right form is part of the right content'.[36] While this is hardly a ringing endorsement of the role of rhetoric, it does

---

34 Willimon, *Conversations with Barth on Preaching*, p. 155.
35 Barth, *Prayer and Preaching*, p. 107.
36 Barth, *Homiletics*, p. 120.

serve as a reminder that matters of form and a care for language and construction do concern Barth and presumably have some role in the revelatory event, or why make the comment?

The fact remains that the preacher, as a communicator, will inevitably make use of rhetorical strategies, consciously or otherwise. How do we develop homiletic strategy that respects the otherness of the revelation of God and at the same time acknowledges the immanence of God who gifts humanity with the potential to speak and to listen? What is the connection between divine providence and human responsibility in the homiletic endeavour? For Barth, God comes to us in his Word by an act of sovereign grace,[37] not because we have alighted on a particular homiletic strategy that means we can have God, fixed and fastened. At the same time preachers need to take responsibility for the nuts and bolts of communicating. This fusion of divine sovereignty and human responsibility means that the preacher is bound to offer their best imaginative listening, preparation and performance. It also means, rather comfortingly, that if because of the limits of our ability, health or time, we can produce little more than a meagre homiletic serving, the grace of God can yet transform the worst of our best efforts into something that brings sustenance.

The preacher as artist

An artist works with a given material; working within a tradition, having trained to gain skills to exercise imagination; performing for an audience within a given context. The purpose of art is to reveal something to the beholder about the world and themselves in relation to that world: 'to open us to that which is hidden, to break open a mystery'.[38] There are clearly potential resonances here between the work of the preacher and that of the artist, if we understand preaching as helping people

37 Willimon, *Conversations with Barth on Preaching*, p. 19.
38 Westerhoff, *Spiritual Life*, p. 23.

to discover truth rather than foisting opinions on them with declamatory certitude. However, without a theological framework this model of the preacher, like that of the teacher, runs the risk of collapsing into over-reliance on human skill alone.

David Trygve, in his PhD thesis exploring the metaphor of preacher as artist, avoids this by helpfully grounding this model in J. B. Torrance's theology of the vicarious work of Christ's one acceptable offering, on behalf of all humanity, in our humanity, to God the Father. United with Christ we are involved in the life of the Trinity through his humanity and his intercessions as High Priest.[39] In Christ, humanity is reconciled to God and God to humanity. The gifts given to us in our humanity – our imagination, creativity and reason – can be offered back to God in Christ, not as a means of strong-arming revelation but as a free response to the revelation we have known. Joined to Christ we are free to exercise our imaginative gifts, free to sing in the lyrical voice, confident that our failings and wrong motivations are known, forgiven and transformed. Freed from homiletic neuroticism, we are enabled to offer all our gifts of imagination, creativity and reason to God in Christ in the preaching event.

Seeing preaching as part of the ongoing creative work of God suggests that we should consider carefully the relational life of the Trinity. In Christ our humanity is invited into the life of the Trinity; in him our redeemed imaginative creativity is employed in the worship of God and the proclamation of God's love. The Spirit guides, leads and nudges us as we seek to engage in the artistry of preaching both as preachers and as hearers. All our preaching endeavours are based on a theology of the Trinity. Given this, the preacher is not to be considered as some tortured artist struggling alone to chisel meaning from the marble of Scripture, but as part of a community, human and divine. The preacher, trusting in God's self-communication, works with Christ, in the collaborative

---

39 J. B. Torrance, *Worship, Community, and the Triune God of Grace*, Downers Grove, IL: InterVarsity Press, 1996, p. 23.

power of the Spirit. They work with the materials of Scripture, life experience, language and performative skill in the context of the gathered community of God's people. Grounded theologically, preachers are free to exercise their imaginative skills fully, without falling into a quagmire of self-reliance. Herein lies part of the joy of preaching. In Christ there is no need to be bound by the 'right' homiletic method. The straitjacketing of such counsels of perfection limits the preacher from offering all of their particular giftedness to God in the task of preaching. Preachers have the freedom to exercise the full stretch of their imaginative skill at the service of the gospel and in fealty to Christ; rooted in this ground, even our preaching 'mistakes' are redeemable.

High up in the quire of Durham Cathedral there is a series of repetitive patterns carved in the shape of an arc. Viewed from left to right we see the arc beginning with an identical series of carvings, uniformly spaced: it is clear that the master craftsman began the work. The stone tells the story of where the apprentice took over. The gaps between the carvings become uneven until, towards the end of the arc, the carvings are squashed in. This looks like the work of a lesser mason, and yet it still speaks of patience and hard work and of a desire to mirror the work of the master. There is something beautiful about this flawed work, which may serve as a metaphor for the preacher as artist bringing together the perfection of the divine artist with the learning of the human apprentice.

Edward Farley asks whether aesthetic art can be taught, as part of his wider discussion concerning whether preaching can be taught. He notes that techniques and styles can be learned but points out that these are not an end in themselves. This leads him to comment that 'there are environments – pedagogical communities and subcultures – that encourage, model, and evoke creativity and imagination'.[40] A key question falls out of this, which concerns how the Church and its

---

40 W. Edward Farley, 'Can Preaching Be Taught?', *Theology Today* 62:2 (2005), p. 176.

training institutions can be communities that actively foster the development and use of the imagination and art in worship and shared common life. One of the key issues over the employment of art in any context is that it requires a willingness to lose control of the interpretation. Communities in which power is located in the hands of a few are not likely to employ art as part of the community's meaning-making, since the interpretation is difficult to control. Imaginative preaching, using the on-look of preacher as artist, will go some way to creating cultures in which the freedom of imagination, issuing forth in creativity, is valued and its links with revelation demonstrated.

There are many positive aspects of the entailments of seeing the preacher as artist. It encourages the preacher to be creative with their homiletic resources, combining methods and models to create new forms. It focuses the preacher on the importance of mastering the craft of preaching as an oral event: being deliberate and thoughtful over structural decisions; language choice and its effects; the use of images; the construction of moves; the nature of movement, delivery and range of vocal intonation. Arguably, a work of art only becomes art when it is exposed to the critical interpretation of its audience. The sermon is only a sermon when preacher and hearer come together to create it. In this model the Church can be seen as a guild of artists, the preacher as a liturgical artist, working with 'other liturgical artists like readers, musicians, visual artists, architects and the artistic mob that is the congregation'.[41] Finally, the preacher as artist model reminds us of the importance of preachers being consciously apprenticed to Christ. Without this there is a danger that the preacher–artist could become self-indulgent, producing pieces that, divorced from the life of the Trinity and the centrality of worship, become empty, self-serving artefacts.

---

41 Trygve, *The Preacher as Artist*, p. 218.

The preacher as jazz musician

A fifth metaphor, which has a number of creative outcomes, is that of the preacher as jazz musician. Jazz has its roots in the African American experience of slavery and oppression that birthed the spirituals and the blues – musical narratives of remembrance, anguish, honesty and hope. The spiritual structure of jazz, with its themes of joy, lament, risk and creative defiance, resonates with the gospel, and these themes are etched into the accounts of Jesus' life. If preaching is to gain a hearing it needs to strike these deep chords in the hearts and minds of hearers. Jazz makes use of improvisation, listening to the 'voices' of others, nuancing, challenging and reworking them creatively in an open-ended movement that seeks to do new things with old notes and riffs. Jazz has a wide range of 'voices'; not least is the capacity to sing the blues with poignancy and healing honesty.

Rigid preaching methods often close down the possibility of improvisation, possibly as a reaction in the preacher to being on the receiving end of experiences of poorly prepared, rambling spiels; and also because for the preacher there is great security in sticking to the script. Jazz teaches us that improvisation has nothing to do with poor preparation. Kirk Byron Jones calls it 'spontaneity infused by preparation'. The preacher who has prepared well, who is familiar with the movement and intent of the sermon score, has the freedom to improvise in the moment, responsive to the other players in the group: the Spirit, the hearers, the Scripture and the sermon script. In this metaphor the sermon script, be it an outline or full notes, might best be seen as a musical score, reminding the preacher of the melodic line should their improvisation need disciplining by the drive and intent of the whole piece. Jones describes the Spirit as the 'Sacred Improvisational Helper', underscoring the importance of listening, risk and trust in the improvised movements of the preaching performance. There is a similar theme here to one raised in the metaphor of preaching as spiritual direction, which is that of listening to other voices in the dialogue. The 'credo of jazz dialogue is this: We are all responsible for and to the music'.[42]

In order to improvise well, the jazz musician practises. Practice is not a dirty word in preaching, although it is rarely mentioned. Rehearsal gives the preacher the confidence to depart from the script, knowing how and where to reconnect with it. This kind of improvisational freedom requires the preacher to relax. Being too uptight and nervous can result in a rigid clinging to the prepared text, often accompanied by the preacher's head dropping down and a consequential loss of eye contact. Such anxiety will communicate itself to the hearer and close down the possibilities of joyous improvisation in the moment.

Jones recounts the following anecdote, reported in the *Atlantic Monthly*, as an illustration of the power of improvisation.[43] The trumpeter Wynton Marsalis was playing at a famous jazz club, the Village Vanguard, in Manhattan. Marsalis is at a low point in his career, playing a supporting role with a lesser known band on a quiet August evening, having lost his record label. At the most dramatic moment of his solo part in 'I Don't Stand a Ghost of a Chance with You', a mobile phone went off in the audience, 'blaring a rapid singsong melody in electronic bleeps. People started giggling and picking up their drinks. The moment – the whole performance – unravelled.' The expectations of the audience were derailed and they turned back to the ordinariness of their conversations. The reporter, David Hajdu, writes in his notebook, 'Magic, Ruined'.[44] The incident seems to reflect the state of Marsalis' career.

However, in a movement filled with profound theological resonance, Marsalis begins to play back the notes of the

---

42 Kirk Byron Jones, *The Jazz of Preaching: How to Preach with Great Freedom and Joy*, Nashville, TN: Abingdon Press, 2004, pp. 85, 94, 102.

43 Jones, *Jazz of Preaching*, p. 79. See also David Hajdu, 'Wynton's Blues', *The Atlantic Webzine* (2003), www.unz.org/Pub/AtlanticWeb-2003mar-00025.

44 Hajdu, 'Wynton's Blues', paragraphs 6 and 7 (no page numbers given).

ringtone, improvising through various keys, slowing down to a ballad tempo and joining the song at exactly the point he left off, finishing in a storm of applause. Marsalis imaginatively weaves the audience member's antisocial oversight into his performance. The 'death' of the performance is swallowed up in the musician's ability to continue through the apparent end point into a renewed, richer performance. Marsalis' improvisation, based on his human skill, wisdom, understanding and courage, combines with a seriously playful defiance. There is an echo of resurrection hope here. God takes the ruin we make of our 'performances' and the damage others inflict and creates the possibility for renewed movement, connected to the old and yet different. Improvisation isn't simply a sermonic technique; it is a theological analogue to the work of God.

With its focus on 'developing a new note disposition',[45] jazz is never satisfied with repeating the same score. Preachers have much to learn from this concept of having a 'new note disposition'. If we accept that the gospel speaks afresh into new situations and is not simply a message to be intoned accurately by an obedient herald, then the preacher needs to attend to the creative process of finding the right notes to allow the music to soar. This entails having a genuine care for words and their weight, being imaginatively open to the way words can operate as sharps and flats, creating resonances and dissonances for particular effects. Developing a new note disposition also reminds the preacher not to be bound to the same sermon structures but to engage with creative and experimental freedom in the quest for a variety of forms that will do new things with old material. This creativity can be seen as a form of worship, taking the best we have to offer and giving it back to God in Christ in the sermon event: herein lies much of the joy of preaching.

Preachers can learn from the blues theme in jazz music. 'Blues preaching is not afraid to hold heartache; it is only after holding it that it walks haltingly onward'.[46] The capacity to name

45 Jones, *Jazz of Preaching*, p. 17.
46 Jones, *Jazz of Preaching*, p. 20.

grief, pain and suffering honestly is one of the entailments of preaching as spiritual direction. One aspect of spiritual direction is the holding of silence, particularly in the presence of the pain of the other. The wordiness of preaching can close down the spaces for the hearer's response. Blues incorporates musical pauses, creating space for the hearer's lament. Blues preaching can effectively hold heartache through honest naming and incorporating silence, creating space for the recognition and expression of emotion. Sermons that are tightly structured, logically ordered edifices can bounce us all too quickly from Good Friday to Easter Sunday; negating the horror of the darkness lessens our appreciation of the joy of the dawn. Preaching can learn from the blues the importance of dwelling in the painful reality of the middle day.

The preacher as jester

Perhaps the best place to begin with this model is by responding to the objections it raises. The jester is another term for the fool, and in both testaments foolishness is opposed to wisdom: the fool is proud, rebellious, greedy and imprudent, as such hardly a fitting subject for emulation. Surely this model denigrates the serious subject matter of Christianity? Is salvation a fitting topic for levity? Doesn't this model of the jester–preacher reduce the *telos* of preaching to mere entertainment? Is there a serious theological foundation underpinning the metaphor of preacher as jester?

On the whole the Scriptures do contrast foolishness with wisdom and condemn the former. Yet Paul plays ironically with the concept of foolishness, particularly in his letters to the Corinthians in which foolishness becomes a matter of perspective.[47] In the cross and its proclamation, God subverts the world's wisdom, confounding human expectation. Human wisdom becomes folly in comparison to the deep wisdom of

---

47 1 Cor. 1.18–31; 2.14; 3.18–19; 4.10; 2 Cor. 11.17–19.

God's foolishness, rooted in the very nature of divine love that cannot be captured or understood by rational calculation. God offers love and in so doing becomes open to rejection, mockery and betrayal, in a move that strikes the fearful, defensive mind as profoundly foolish. Yet the foolishness of divine love does that which 'all the ingenuity of wisdom cannot. It can turn evil into good'.[48] For the person who seeks to live in the strength of this foolish love, new possibility arises in the freedom of forgiveness received and offered. This sense of the foolishness of God is earthed in the person of Christ.

Harvey Cox identifies aspects of the jester in the life of Christ, who defies custom, scorns kings and, like a wandering troubadour, fraternizes with questionable characters. In entering Jerusalem on a donkey in mock pageantry, Christ satirizes authority, a satire ironically echoed in the way the soldiers attire him in the paraphernalia of royalty.[49] If the story ended with the burial of Jesus, this mock pageantry would be painful and tragic. However, the resurrection turns the Christian faith into divine comedy, and comedy is the language of laughter and hope. The resurrection relativizes all that has come before. The mourning of Mary, as an archetype of all who suffer, is utterly transformed. In the serious business in that garden, in the early morning light, surely laughter rings out across eternity? On this basis, salvation is a most fitting subject for levity!

The jester's role is irrevocably associated with comedy, which while associated with the generation of laughter, has a much broader framework; the comic sermon is not to be judged by the degree of laughter it generates. Joseph Webb offers five aspects of the comedic spirit.[50] First, he identifies immanence in the comic vision, a point also made by Cox: 'Comedy disports

---

48 John Austin Baker, *The Foolishness of God*, London: Darton, Longman & Todd, 1970, p. 402.

49 Harvey Cox, *The Feast of Fools: A Theological Essay on Festivity and Fantasy*, Cambridge, MA: Harvard University Press, 1969, pp. 140–1.

50 Joseph Webb, *Comedy and Preaching*, St Louis, MO: Chalice Press, 1998, pp. 21–34.

in the mud and gumminess of life, it has no pretensions'.[51] Undoubtedly both are right to highlight the comedic focus on the earthy and ordinary, but this underplays the comic potential in the interplay between the eternal and the everyday, which cashes out in the rich theology of the divine comedy mentioned above.

Second, he points to the probing doubt of comedy, which opens up authority through question, parody and bold naming. The jester can be seen as a form of institutionalized doubt whose job it is to poke fun at the pomp and ceremony of the court. Sadly, too often the preacher is a representative of this pomp and ceremony, failing to see the connection, at least in the Anglican Church, between their clerical garb and the jester's motley. Perhaps an argument for the wearing of vestments is to keep the preacher in touch with the comic holiness of their vocation.

In an essay on *King Lear*, L. C. Knights writes that:

> The Fool . . . speaks to (and out of) a quite different order of apprehension: his function is to disturb with glimpses of confounding truths that elude rational formulation.[52]

This captures something of the role of the preacher. The gospel intersects with the everyday in its 'confounding truths' of judgement, forgiveness, grace and hope, which do 'elude rational formulation'. Lear's Fool demonstrates courage and wit. He sees and names boldly the rapacious behaviour of Lear's daughters, Goneril and Regan, and wittily chastises Lear for the folly of trying to make 'his daughters his mothers', noting that in so doing Lear 'gavest them the rod, and put'st down thine own breeches'.[53] The Fool demonstrates foresight and understanding, reading the truth of the situation he interprets

---

51 Cox, *Feast of Fools*, p. 150.

52 L. C. Knights, *Some Shakespearian Themes*, London: Chatto & Windus, 1959, p. 108.

53 *King Lear*, Act 1, scene IV, 179–81.

to Lear. Speaking boldly from a position of powerlessness, the Fool runs the risk of being whipped for his words. Truth-telling is a serious and costly undertaking which, perhaps, only a fool would undertake. Preaching in the footsteps of the Divine Fool will find preachers speaking words of dangerous wisdom. The jester's role is to question that which seems self-evident. We see Jesus doing exactly this in many of his encounters and parables. For example, it is self-evident to the Pharisee that the woman anointing Jesus' feet is a worthless sinner (Luke 7.36–50); it is clear to the disciples that the storm will kill them (Mark 4.38–40), and to the crowds that Zacchaeus is a thieving rogue (Luke 19.1–9). In each case Jesus discloses the 'more' in the situation. Cox reminds us that 'the clown refuses to live inside this present reality'.[54] On the basis of resurrection hope, the jester–preacher, 'a fool for Christ's sake' (1 Cor. 4.10), must resist all attempts to normalize, neutralize or dismiss the radical, surprising, hope-filled resonances of the resurrection.

Third, Webb highlights the identification of incongruity as a hallmark of comedic vision. 'This is the comedy created when disparities or even conflicts within an individual or social order are made explicit and held up for public scrutiny'.[55] In preaching this can involve the naming of conflicts within biblical characters as a way of holding up a mirror to our own hypocrisy and conflict: David the great king portrayed as a peeping Tom; Elijah who called down fire, huddled in a miasma of depression; or Judas, a chosen disciple, clutching his bag of tainted silver. Comic recognition here is not designed to elicit laughter but is deployed as a penitential lure.

Fourth, Webb highlights how the comedic spirit of ambiguity messes up clearly drawn lines, muddling the neat separation between insiders and outsiders that always grants the moral high ground to the powerful insider. Jesus challenges this attitude from the start of his ministry, pointing out that the grace of God is not the preserve of Israel, it extends to Sidonians and

---

54 Cox, *Feast of Fools*, p. 150.
55 Webb, *Comedy and Preaching*, p. 25.

Syrians (Luke 4.25–27). In our preaching is there ever a tendency to draw neat and tidy lines around those who are regarded as on God's team and those who are not? Do we expect to find grace on the 'wrong side of the tracks'? The preacher informed by the comedic vision will be open to the divine inversion of our theology, which may find good Christian folk cheek by jowl with the Pharisee, and the woman of dubious reputation given a seat at top table.

Finally, and related to the last point, Webb comments that the 'goal and end of classic comedy' is 'invariably social equality and solidarity'.[56] This involves the bringing down of the high up and the raising of the low, which brings to mind the dynamics of the Magnificat. Comic vision seems to underpin the social inversions inherent in this divine agenda. Ultimately, the comic vision presses those who think they are above the common fray into the realization of our interconnectedness, which, in shared laughter, challenges loneliness and alienation.

Suggesting that the preacher inhabits the jester's motley might be seen to reduce the *telos* of preaching to mere entertainment. The word 'entertainment' is problematic as it carries connotations of the superficial and idle, a mere time-killing pastime, to tickle the fancy. Entertainment is associated with consumption and with pleasing the recipient; given this, the idea that the final goal of preaching is entertainment is anathema. However, one of Cicero's aims for oratory, which Augustine applies to preaching, is to delight the hearer, and such delight is associated with persuasion – moving the hearer to a different perspective and action. Any teacher knows that the best way to capture the imagination of the learner and generate interest in the subject is to make it interesting, engaging and, dare I say it, entertaining. This is far from a view of entertainment as mere frippery; for something to truly captivate it needs to ignite our hearts with its compelling importance. In this sense entertaining the hearer might be seen as a doorway, not an end point.

---

56 Webb, *Comedy and Preaching*, p. 27.

It is a means of engaging the hearer tied in with the deeper purpose of moving them.

However, if the only aim is to generate laughter to create a feel-good mood, pandering to the preacher's desire to be liked, then that should and must be ruled offside. With that in mind, the use of jokes in the pulpit, especially the practice of starting with a joke, especially one culled from a book of sermon jokes, should be questioned, particularly if there is no connection between the content of the joke and the purpose of the sermon. The danger in beginning with a joke, particularly one that has no thematic connection to the body of the sermon, is that it can set up a false contract with the hearer. The joke presents one register, often at odds with the register of the main body of the sermon. Warren Wiersbe comments that 'If humour is natural to the preacher, then it should be used in preaching; but one must never "import" jokes just to make the congregation laugh'.[57] Preachers need to be themselves. If they have a gift for humour, then that will naturally shape the way they preach. If they don't, then importing off-the-shelf jokes will usually fail, at worst generating the deathly titter of insincere laughter. Often such jokes have little to do with the sermon, and irritate and patronize with the inherent assumption that congregations need 'warming up'. Congregations do give their attention to the preacher at the outset: the preacher's task is to hold it.

The comedic vision of preaching scrapes away the superficiality of the imported joke and has the potential to truly grip us. Does this mean that sermons should evoke laughter? Much depends on the nature of the laughter evoked. Derisive, sarcastic mockery has no place in preaching. The 'horrid laughter of the oppressor'[58] may be named, but never evoked. However, preaching that evokes the laughter of self-identification and recognition binds the hearers together affectively. This is the holy, joyous laughter of the community of sinners who know

---

57 Warren Wiersbe, *Preaching and Teaching with Imagination: The Quest for Biblical Ministry*, Grand Rapids: MI, Baker Books, 1994, p. 275.
58 Webb, *Comedy and Preaching*, p. 12.

who they are and who Christ is, and who can always look forward in hope, even when that laughter is accompanied by tears of penitence and grief.

The preacher can learn a great deal from the work of our contemporary jesters on the stand-up scene. Successful comics demonstrate observational imagination, communicative body language, apparent spontaneity and the ability to interact with their audiences. Looking at the work of Peter Kay and Michael McIntyre, in particular, we see that their comedy is drawn from their keen observational skill. They notice the oddities of life, from our scripted chit-chat with taxi drivers – 'Been on long? What time do you finish?' – to the politics of the contents of the condiment cupboard. They have keenly attuned sensory imaginations that notice, question and highlight. We laugh because we recognize our life and behaviour in their observations. The preacher as jester needs to notice the oddities of our human behaviour in the ordinary stuff of life.

Eddie Izzard is a master of facial expression and gesture. In the riff 'Engelbert Humperdinck is Dead' he is able to repeatedly contradict and confirm the singer's death. He raises his eyebrows, opens his eyes wide, nods his head to indicate the truth of the statement and then frowns, shakes his head, sometimes accompanied by a palm-down gesture of the hand, to deny the statement. At the height of the gag, he uses no words, his body shifts are minimal, but they communicate his intent clearly and carry the audience with him.[59] In 'Cats and Dogs' his body movement and gestures create a sense of narrative space; the audience know exactly where the sofa is and where the cat is in relation to the owner and the visiting neighbour. His use of gesture to demonstrate the cat putting on its goggles and drilling adds comic texture to the piece.[60] The mimes are simple and effective and demonstrate to preachers how body position, varied eyelines and gesture can create a sense of a story inhabiting a space. By changing body stance the preacher

---

59 Eddie Izzard, www.youtube.com/watch?v=LMU9wUHSapc.
60 Eddie Izzard, www.youtube.com/watch?v=zOqQ4hEPp1I./

can become a different character and create a sense of holding a conversation with another character. Study of any effective contemporary comedian demonstrates the importance of apparent spontaneity, which takes a great deal of practice. Preachers often invest considerable time in working up a sermon text but sometimes fail to consider how to get the text off the page and end up simply reading the text to their hearers. This hampers the development of a sense of relational 'togetherness' in the preaching event. This is not to argue for or against having a sermon script, rather to make the point that the preacher needs to be familiar enough with the content to be free to paraphrase, look up, move about and make use of gesture.

There is a balance to be struck between having a care for language and becoming trapped by a written text. The key, as all good dramatists, poets, comedians, speech writers and liturgists know, is to write for the ear. A problem many new preachers encounter is not that they write their script out in full – which is a good discipline – but they write it as an essay, forgetting that the hearer does not have the reader's opportunity to scan back up the page. The preacher needs to attend carefully to language that paints an impression for the hearer, being open to inspiration in all stages of the sermon, from crafting on the page to inhabiting it in context. Careful preparation is vital but the preacher needs not to be so text-dependent that there is no space for interacting with the hearers in the event of the sermon: picking up on the mood of the moment and risking some improvisation.

The goal is a combination of care for crafted language and a genuine presence in the preaching moment. Effective comedians engage with their audiences, making the live event a one-off, weaving the ad lib into the performance script. Similarly, the effective preacher needs to be in touch with the hearers during the sermon, making eye contact, alert to their responses in body language and attentive to the mood the sermon creates.

Considering the on-look of preacher as jester reminds the preacher that Christianity is essentially a comedy, founded on hope. Preaching itself is a kind of foolish wisdom in which preachers do well to take the task with utmost seriousness and themselves with somewhat more levity. This model is associated with bold speech, naming truth to power and respecting the hearers' need to be genuinely engaged. There is something profoundly joyful in this model of preaching, which has such an appealing authenticity about it. In an age of cynicism and mistrust, 'the human community needs a company of dreamers, seers, servants, and jesters in its midst'.[61]

The images of the preacher analysed in this chapter are not meant to be exhaustive. The intention here has been to show how the metaphors that master us shape our practice and to highlight the need for preachers to be encouraged to become conscious of how they imagine the preaching task and to explore how this perspective affects their praxis. Adopting new metaphors for the preaching task can bring new approaches and richer theological understanding of the purposes and methods of preaching. So we see that imagination is at work in the conception of preaching as well as in the creation of the sermon. Once again the point becomes clear: imagination is vital to preaching.

---

61 Webb, *Comedy and Preaching*, p. 96.

6

Lighting the Blue Touch-Paper – Implications for the Practice and Teaching of Preaching

Finally, we arrive at the all-important question: 'And so what?' If imagination is vital to preaching, what does this mean for the preacher? The basic premise is that imagination is a gift that is shaped by the way we develop it. While the key time for imaginative development is in childhood and adolescence, it can also be developed in adulthood.

> If we conceive of the imagination as a power or capacity we all possess at least in nascent form, then analogous to a virtue such as patience, it becomes strengthened through practice.[1]

Frederick Buechner compares imagination to muscles that 'can be strengthened through practice and exercise'.[2] Highlighting the importance of developing imagination, Anna Carter Florence uses the same image: 'Imagination is not an ingredient you add in. It is a muscle you develop'.[3] The entire premise of

1 Sandra M. Levy, *Imagination and the Journey of Faith*, Grand Rapids, MI: Eerdmans, 2008, p. 115.

2 Frederick Buechner, *Whistling in the Dark*, San Francisco: Harper, 1993, p. 69.

3 Anna Carter Florence, 'The Preaching Imagination', in *Teaching Preaching as a Christian Practice*, ed. Thomas G. Long and Nora Tubbs Tisdale, Louisville, KY: Westminster John Knox Press, 2008, pp. 123, 116–33.

Eric Liu and Scott Noppe-Brandon's helpful secular book on developing imagination is that 'imagination is completely malleable: we all have it – and we can all develop it'.[4]

Reflecting on the themes explored in the previous chapters and based on this premise, three important conclusions emerge. First, the exercise of imagination is an important spiritual discipline for the preacher. Second, the preacher needs to engage with the imagination in each of its four functions throughout the sermonic process. Third, imagination frees the preacher to look at their role in a variety of ways and risk trying new sermonic structures and performance methods, having assessed what might be most appropriate in a given context. Developing such imaginative preachers has implications for teaching homiletics, relating to the teacher's engagement with the students and the nature of curriculum design.

Mystery and the mundane: developing imagination as a spiritual discipline

It is from the basis of developing imagination as a spiritual discipline that genuinely profound connection can be made between mystery and the mundane. If we are to notice God in the everyday, to make connections, seeing this as that, we need to be imaginatively open and alert. Robert H. McKim comments that 'any mental ability that is not exercised decays'. He makes a connection between perceptual loss and lost imagination.[5] Although he is not writing from a faith perspective, his point is instructive. The role of the sensory imagination is to notice and to gather data. However, many of us run our lives with the accelerator foot so heavy on the pedal that we do not really attend to the richness of sensory details in the world around

---

4 Eric Liu and Scott Noppe-Brandon, *Imagination First: Unlocking the Power of Possibility*, San Francisco: Wiley, 2009, p. 22.

5 Robert H. McKim, *Experiences in Visual Thinking*, Belmont, CA: Wadsworth, 1972, p. 24.

us; our sensory imagination operates only passively. Clergy often find sermon preparation time squeezed by the multiple demands of ministry. Likewise, lay preachers can be pressured by the demands of their working lives and family commitments. If preaching is to have depth and resonance, the preacher needs to develop their sensory imagination as a spiritual discipline, resisting the lure of worthy busyness.

Genuine seeing, as opposed to superficial, passive skimming, is an art we need to develop actively. The same can be said for hearing, tasting, touching and smelling. Preachers need to be encouraged to really focus on exercising sensory imagination as they engage with the details of the everyday and walk the landscape of Scripture with the senses alert. Herein is a gateway to experiencing wonder and joy and the route into noticing the suffering of the other. Unless preachers attend to the details of the everyday, how can we ever really understand and preach into the contexts within which we are located? A stunted sensory imagination offers little to the other functions of imagination, resulting in vapid description that does not resonate with the hearers' context, lack of precision, weak affective connection and a paucity of detailed data to offer to the intellectual imaginative function. How might such sensory awareness be promoted?

Developing contemplation

One key method is in encouraging the preacher to slow down and notice, to develop a contemplative and sacramental aware-ness. Sandra Levy makes the point that exhaustion, distraction and laziness are obstacles to imagination.[6] With this in mind, preachers need to be encouraged to pause, whether that is the deliberate pause of the scheduled retreat or the regular recollec-tion of the self before God in the midst of a busy day. Liu and Noppe-Brandon observe that 'modern life is almost completely

---

6 Levy, *Imagination and the Journey of Faith*, p. 118.

free of stillness'.[7] The contemplative practice of stillness leads to greater attention to the sights, sounds, smells and textures of the everyday, providing a rich data bank for the preacher.

Related to this need to slow down is the irrevocable connection between the state of the body and our ability to imagine. As embodied beings, if we are tensed up, tired or run-down our imaginative insight is distracted. Many preachers might be relieved to learn that all work and no play makes for poor preaching. Preaching preparation crammed into the last minute will suffer, since there is no relaxed opportunity for the intuitive imagination to play with the material, nor for affective reflection and the logical working of the intellectual imaginative process.

Radical openness: engagement with the imagination throughout the sermonic process

Ignatian meditation

Ignatian meditation on scriptural passages can contribute to a rich sensory reading of the text. This practice works particularly well with narrative text. It invites us to locate ourselves within the passage, noting details of the unfolding scene with the eye of imagination. It helps to allow the account to roll like a film within which you are a character. What do we see and from what perspective? What is the soundscape of the narrative? What can we smell, touch and taste? Exploring such questions helps the preacher to inhabit the narrative and enable others to step into it. With imagination on high alert we can focus in on characters, noting details of their speech and action, guided by the text as a guard against rewriting the story. Ignatian meditation on Scripture helps the reader to notice details they might otherwise have missed. It is particularly effective with very familiar passages, where our familiarity can lead us to

---

7 Liu and Noppe-Brandon, *Imagination First*, pp. 43–5.

skim-read, reinforcing old readings and inhibiting new seeing. Ignatian techniques slow us down and create space for pondering the details of the biblical narratives. In such imaginative reflection new perspectives and understandings often emerge. Imaginative techniques can also work with non-narrative texts. Biblical texts are written against a narrative backdrop – the story that brought the text into being and the context in which it was written. Exploring that story and trying to hear the text with the ears of its first audience can give a richer reading and is a deeply imaginative undertaking.

Changing on-looks

Our on-looks condition how we see others and ourselves in the world. Our perceptual filter affects our vision but sometimes our on-looks are so engrained we barely notice them. With a different filter we see anew and different questions arise. When we engage the sensory imagination, how do we interpret what we see? Do I see the drunken tramp as a dangerous threat, a social embarrassment or a child of God? Such imaginative refocusing challenges our stereotyped on-look habits. This is what Jesus demonstrates in his seeing, which challenged culturally conditioned stereotypes: a tax collector is seen as a son of Abraham and religious professionals as a hindrance to the spiritual growth of the people.[8] What we 'see' when we look on without question are socially conditioned stereotypes. To become aware of such distorted seeing and increase awareness of the danger of our snap judgements, 'deferring the blink' is a useful exercise for preachers:

> The work of cultivating imagination is, in some respects, the work of deferring the blink – keeping eyes pried open – and suspending the process of judgement formation.[9]

---

8 Luke 19.9; Matt. 23.13.
9 Liu and Noppe-Brandon, *Imagination First*, p. 115.

For the preacher, deferring the blink means not assuming we have seen all there is to see in the text and the local context. In withholding judgement there is space to explore our perceptions and ask what we are not seeing in the way we frame the world. Deferring the blink can mean asking where I have positioned myself in the biblical text. Do I naturally identify with the good and the righteous, or am I with the sinner? Deferring the blink means reading the text as if for the first time, being willing to set aside my sense of familiarity and being expectant for new insights to emerge. If the Scripture breathes anew into new contexts then we need to learn to set aside prized interpretations and look again.

Attending to the 'in-press' of ideas

Attending to the intuitive imagination requires that preachers give time for the 'in-press' of ideas before they turn to efforts to express. The in-press process can be fed by allowing the intuitive imagination to make its connective leaps and giving a free rein to curiosity without censorship. Often potentially interesting ideas can be closed down by an inner critic waving an offside flag: 'That's a silly idea'; 'This doesn't make sense'; 'You can't ask that question.' Gently mugging the inner critic creates space to play, wonder and ponder without worrying about quite what the end result will be. Openness to drawing connections with the biblical text from everyday life, both high and low culture, without closing down possibilities through a misguided sense of piety, will lead to much richer and deeper ideas. Such openness is a result of a deep sacramental understanding of God's engagement with the world, both playful and childlike. This is echoed by Barbara Brown Taylor, who offers this beautiful extended simile to capture her sense of the playfulness of the imagination:

> Imagination is like a child roaming the neighbourhood on a free afternoon, following first the smell of fresh bread in an

oven, then the glint of something bright in the grass – led by curiosity, by hunger, by hope, to explore the world. When imagination comes home and empties its pockets, of course there will be some sorting to do. But do not scold imagination for bringing it all home or for collecting it in the first place.[10]

Taylor's image of the child roaming the neighbourhood is deeply evocative, giving a powerful and appealing sense of ludic freedom and joy; regarding imagination as a source of discovery without judgement.

There are many ways for the preacher to bring to birth the fruit of intuitive engagement and provide further material with which the imagination can play. Pondering with a pen can help to spark initial ideas. Scribbling notes freely and doodling is a kind of creative play that shapes ideas on the page. In the process of sketching out thoughts, in words or in images, the imagination is given opportunities to shape and refine the material. Often in the first reading of a passage particular words leap off the page. Jotting these down can ensure that early thoughts and ideas are not overshadowed or lost. Asking quirky offbeat questions can kick-start the intuitive imagination into making connections: 'What music could I set this text to and why?' Another way in is to imagine painting the unfolding mood of the text: 'What colours would I use and why?' 'What other biblical texts come to mind in the light of the one I am focused on?' Often a thread emerges leading to some rummaging around in the Bible. Scripture comes to interpret and illuminate Scripture. Sketching out the geography and movement of a biblical passage can give a sense of how the text is operating, where the climactic moment is and how and if resolution is reached. Drawing speech bubbles to record what characters say on one side of the page, with thought bubbles exploring what they might be thinking on the opposite side,

10 Barbara Brown Taylor, *The Preaching Life*, Norwich: Canterbury Press, 2013, p. 51.

can help re-centre the preacher's viewpoint and generate empathy. Listing responses to the passage, the preacher's own and the imagined responses of the hearer, without airbrushing out difficult questions or reactions, will contribute to a sermon with integrity and punch rather than the insipid offering that paddles in the waters of the blindingly obvious. Drawing out the sermon shape, blocking out sermonic moves, can help to ensure that sermon structure and content support each other. Playing with words on the page, exploring the sensory potential of lyrical description, while resisting the pressure to move too quickly from jotted notes to a more developed script, can give freedom to the intuitive function to practise writing for the ear.

Attending to the wisdom of Atticus

Working with the affective imaginative function calls the preacher to explore their sympathetic and empathetic connections with biblical characters and adopt the perspectives of potential hearers of the sermon. Following the wisdom of Atticus Finch (see Chapter 1), the imaginative preacher will step into the skin of different hearers, seeking to establish trust through the development of affective bonds. This calls for genuine attention to be paid to the details of people's life stories and contexts. Sermons that seek to engage the imagination of hearers will create spaces, ask open-ended questions and invite hearers to make the sermon their own. Care needs to be exercised to ensure that images and instances and illustrative material are not all drawn from the same sphere of life – this shows a failure to consider the range of experiences of the hearers and reduces the potential for affective engagement across the congregation. There are only so many football references the average congregation can take!

The affectively imaginative preacher will look outward and ask questions about the other's experience of the world. How is it to struggle with an angry two-year-old in a supermarket aisle under a collective judgemental 'tut'? How does it feel to find a job after years of unemployment? What is the experience of the frailty of old age like, when physical confidence has been shaken by falls? To ensure that preaching does not become overly parochial and inward-looking, imagination needs to be tuned into the details of narratives beyond our immediate horizons. This will involve a high regard for the humanity of the other – friend or enemy, near or far away. Engagement with reports in the media needs to happen with the eyes of the heart wide open, wondering and questioning. Even if the preacher can never fully grasp the experience of living in exile, of growing up in a civil war, of losing someone in a disaster, failure to try to stand in the shoes of the other is a failure of love. The affective function of imagination reminds us that neighbour love extends beyond the borders of nation and the boundaries of background. Herein is the route to humaneness and humility without which the gospel becomes distorted into a parochial short-sighted mantra for individualistic well-being. Preaching must challenge this distortion by bringing in the experience of the other, keeping the eyes of our imaginations focused well beyond the horizons of the church walls.

Applying suppositional 'if . . . then'

Intellectual imagination in preaching follows the logic of eschatological hope, structured around the Easter faith that the hopelessness of Friday's death and desolation will be redeemed in the light of Sunday's resurrection. It is this faithful, determined hope that gives the strength to endure the long Saturday. Intellectual imagination can sustain the weary emotions and the darkened intuition with an insistent grasp on the hypothesis that 'If God has promised redemption, *then* redemption will come'. This gives courage and strengthens the lyrical voice to give wing to words in the heart of darkness and desolation, renaming and reimagining as a source of hope.

Theological coherence will also be a concern for the intellectually imaginative preacher, generating a number of questions. Is the drive of the biblical text at odds with other biblical passages? Is the drive of the sermon in line with orthodoxy? Are their voices in the tradition that would support or conflict with the view expressed in the sermon?

Blocking out the stages of the argument can help the preacher to shape logical development and clear stages, ensuring that each sermon move flows into the next. This practice will also enable the preacher to anticipate and respond to congregational objection: 'If x is argued then y might be the objection. The response to y is to suggest z'. Naming and responding to the congregational objection is an important aspect of imagination in preaching. As a hearer it is engaging and disarming to hear your objections named, treated with respect and care and afforded a plausible response.

The intellectual imagination can act as a watchdog on the affective imagination which, with its concern for the feelings of the other, can peddle cheap grace, blunting the prophetic edge of the sermon and muting the ethical challenge of the gospel. The prophetic thrust of the intellectual imagination is not afraid to push the challenge: '*If* we believe, trust and love God, *then* our behaviour will reflect an orientation around God and not self'. '*If* our behaviour does not demonstrate such gospel values, *then* what does it demonstrate?' Unimpeded by an over-concern for the feeling of the hearer, the intellectual imagination can give the preacher courage to speak hard truths.

Intellectual imagining can help the preacher reflect on performative method. This might involve picturing the preaching space and exploring issues related to sightlines, acoustics, the formal/informal nature of the context and congregational expectations, before making sermonic decisions on an 'if . . . then' basis. Here the preacher can usefully engage imaginative supposition to explore the possible results of deliberately seeking to preach in ways that challenge and surprise expectation. For example:

- If the sermon were preached from a place other than the usual space, what might the effect be?
  - Would the closeness of preaching from the aisle be experienced as welcome or too intimate?
- Could the sermon be hooked around a sung response from a familiar hymn, asking the congregation to join in the refrain?
  - What effect might this achieve?
  - Would it increase a sense of congregational togetherness?
- If projected visuals were incorporated into this sermon, what might the benefit be?
  - At what cost?
- Could another voice be part of the sermon?
- Could the sermon set up questions for congregational discussion within the event of the sermon?
- Would the congregation 'play'?

Such questions demonstrate a willingness to try new ideas, openness to the potential of failure as a stage in deeper learning and a desire to connect deeply with the hearers.

Develop a repertoire: trying new sermonic structures and performance methods

Linked to the discussion above, being wedded to one particular style of sermon structure and delivery betrays a lack of imaginative reflection and perhaps a lack of confidence. Sermon structure and delivery are theological issues and it is important that preachers ask themselves what their favoured preaching styles communicate theologically and whether this is in itself theologically limiting. A useful imaginative practice is to 'unschool yourself periodically',[11] recognizing that the point of achieving mastery is not to stamp out repeated performance ad infinitum but rather to have the courage and confidence to master new approaches. As preachers develop competency in their craft,

---

11 Liu and Noppe-Brandon, *Imagination First*, pp. 176–9.

they can afford to take risks and develop new methods, not for the sake of novelty but to be faithful to the scriptural shape and purpose and the nature of the context. Very often, preaching in a liturgical context results in a lack of variety in the shape of the sermon and its relationship to the rest of the liturgy. Predictability can foster boredom. Imaginative preachers are open to the new-note disposition of jazz.

Preachers can learn much from the use of 'placement' in British Sign Language, in which the narrator of a story indicates through sign, gesture and eye movement where the people and objects they are describing are located, using the body to narrate the space. Employing this technique, the preacher can implicitly locate the congregation within the geography of the narrative. They are no longer distant observers but players in the game – an effect that reduces emotional distance. This requires the preacher to be aware of their position in the narrative. For example, in preaching on the story of Zacchaeus, seeking to inhabit and offer commentary on the narrative, is the preacher below the tree, looking up, or in the position of Zacchaeus looking down? It might be that during the sermon flow the preacher wishes to change characters. This can be enacted with a change of the angle of the head and a shift in eyeline. In this way the preacher can indicate conversational shifts.

Rather than repeating the same sermon structure and delivery week in and week out, the imaginative preacher will develop a repertoire of methods and skills, always focused on using these to work with God in effecting encounter and transformation in the sacramental event of the sermon. Using the word 'repertoire' might offend some, linking preaching with acting or pretence. On the contrary, preaching is about integrity and honesty, but this needs to be communicated in some way, and all communication is a form of performance, the bringing of something to expression. The question facing the preacher concerns discerning the best performative method to convey the sermonic content with the greatest truth. Here preachers need to be true to Scripture, true to the context and true to themselves. Hence a repertoire of preaching methods and performance skills is profoundly helpful. To this end it is worth remembering that the richest repertoire resides not in the individual but in the preaching team. Imaginative preaching is best achieved through a team of people offering the best of their repertoire on a rota basis. Too often all the preaching rests with one person, which is a recipe for burnout and congregational boredom.

Within some contexts this may raise the objection that many ministers serve in areas where there are no other preachers, one minister perhaps covering a number of churches, perhaps working in deprived areas where people lack the confidence or biblical literacy to begin to preach. This situation requires an imaginative response that seeks to give people confidence. Possibilities could include designing a sermon series that includes opportunities for people to share their stories, working with the preacher to weave this into the sermon. Another way of building confidence is through preaching preparation and response groups. Part of the role of the imaginative preacher is drawing from the ordinary theology of the people, recognizing potential preachers in the congregation, signposting them to training opportunities and offering encouragement and support.

Implications for homiletics teaching

In response to the disclaimer 'I don't have any imagination', Robert McKim suggests that the main difficulty is not a lack of imagination but an inability to contact imagination consciously and exercise it productively.[12] If imagination is a gift given, which can be nurtured and shaped to help us to apprehend the divine, then it should be a vital element in theological education.

Theological education is a place for naming God and naming God is an act of the imagination. Theological colleges and seminaries must be places that foster, encourage and equip the imagination. We can do this by creating an environment

---

12 McKim, *Experiences in Visual Thinking*, p. 25.

within the institution sympathetic to, and encouraging of, the development of the imaginative expression.[13]

How do theological institutions achieve this? A full answer would require an entire book! At the very least, preaching within the worship of the institution needs to model an imaginative approach, avoiding the pitfall of assuming that theological students and staff need, want or even like heavyweight theological lectures in the place of the sermon. This is not an argument for dumbing down the intellectual weight of the sermon, rather a call to preach deep, profound and thoughtful sermons that are daring, artistic and risky. One of the ways to inculcate new vision is to show rather than tell. Given this, the powerful potential of the sermon needs to be demonstrated in the preaching happening in theological institutions.

Furthermore, if imagination is central to preaching then the homiletics classroom needs to be a place that particularly fosters, encourages and equips students' imaginations. In a paper on the status of imagination in secondary school English teaching, Lisa Dart makes the observation that the imaginative engagement of the teacher fosters the development of the children's imaginative response.[14] Similarly, teachers of homiletics need to model imaginative engagement in the way they approach the subject of preaching. Imagination needs to be part of the cargo of the preaching curriculum, a subject for theological discussion in its own right. It is also the vehicle that enables the communication and reception of curriculum content. Whatever else it might be, the homiletics classroom should never be dull. If it is to inspire spiritual discipline, theological faithfulness, rich scriptural engagement, openness to the sacramental nature of life, a willingness to play with language and risk performance, then the teaching of preaching *must* be rooted in imagination.

---

13 Douglas Purnell, 'Educating the Whole Body: Addressing and Equipping the Imagination in Theological Education', *Pastoral Psychology* 49:3 (2001), p. 219.

14 Lisa Dart, 'Literacy and the Lost World of the Imagination', *Educational Research* 43:1 (2001), p. 68.

A number of issues flow from this in terms of engagement with students and curriculum design.

In terms of engagement with students, the affectively imaginative teacher will be aware of the potential range of emotions present, particularly as a new class forms. The potential for fear and vulnerability in adult learners, particularly those new to preaching, is very high. Those who have had prior preaching experience may feel a sense of defensiveness about being required to take a preaching class and are likely to come with a desire to prove themselves as competent preachers, which may impede their openness to learning new homiletic methods. The affectively imaginative teacher will be sensitive to the unnamed anxieties in the room and aware of their importance. Such emotions are not merely to be named and then dismissed or avoided.[15] Fear, anxiety, vulnerability and defensiveness are theologically important in the practice of preaching, partly as they remind us of the foolishness of the undertaking and our inherent need of God. Such emotions need to be articulated and then managed if students are to be free to engage with the curriculum content with serious playfulness.

Dart makes the point that 'A climate where approaches of "play", "experiment" and "risk-taking", which it is well recognized often leads to creative outcomes, needs to be established and valued'.[16] The same holds true in the homiletics class, where serious playfulness demands taking risks and being prepared to fail as part of the learning process. Indeed, Liu and Noppe-Brandon hold up failing well as an imaginative practice that runs counter to the fear of getting it wrong and looking a fool.[17] Students who do not feel that the environment is safe will not try new things – a reluctance that will hamper their development as preachers. In establishing relationship with a

---

15 For an exploration of the importance of attending to emotion in adult education, see John M. Dirkx, 'The Power of Feelings: Emotion, Imagination, and the Construction of Meaning in Adult Learning', *New Directions for Adult and Continuing Education* 89 (2001), pp. 63–72.

16 Dart, 'Literacy and the Lost World of the Imagination', p. 72.

17 Liu and Noppe-Brandon, *Imagination First*, pp. 186–91.

preaching class, the teacher will seek to create a safe space for anxiety to be acknowledged, explored and understood.

Imaginative strategies to manage these emotions may include the use of humour, the use of story – the teacher sharing their own anxieties in their preaching – and the provision of opportunities for the naming of experiences and anxieties in non-threatening ways. Examples of the last might include students working to create a tableau, such as 'My Sunday morning congregation', to draw out expression and discussion of students' understanding of their preaching contexts and the challenges these create. Getting students to work together to name their hopes and fears as preachers can help to create a sense of shared journey and lessen the fear through the act of shared naming. A 'cross-the-space' exercise can help students see the range of backgrounds and experiences in the group, students crossing the space if they, for example, read news online, watch soap operas, listen to local radio and so on. A spectrum exercise can help to draw out the variety of opinions and experiences students have concerning preaching. Students are asked to arrange themselves in a line in response to a range of questions, with 'strongly agree' and 'strongly disagree' at opposite ends of the spectrum.[18] Questions might include 'Should sermons always be preached on one biblical text?', 'Do women preach differently from men?' or 'Does it matter what you wear when you preach?' The benefit of the spectrum exercise is that it creates a physical representation of the variety of ideas in the room. Once the students have decided on their position in response to the question, the teacher can draw out their thinking and create discussion, encouraging a respect for diversity and pushing students to think critically and reflectively.

The affectively imaginative teacher will also be sensitive to possible student resistance to a focus on imagination in preaching, and might respond to this through creating the opportunity

---

18 These three exercises were designed by David Wilkinson as part of the first session in a preaching course at Cranmer Hall, St John's College, Durham.

for students to engage theologically with the framework of imaginative function. Doing the 'describe imagination to an alien' exercise (see Chapter 1) and grouping student responses into the sensory, intuitive, affective, intellectual grid can help to give a sense of coherence around the variety of definitions students will offer. The framework of imaginative function is a heuristic tool to enable discussion of imagination in the homiletics classroom. Inevitably, some definitions may overlap areas, but broadly speaking responses that deal with forming inner pictures belong in the sensory imagination and responses that connect imagination to daydreaming – and the sudden leaps and insights that come in a rush – belong in the intuitive category. Ideas that link imagination with appreciating another's feeling state lie under the affective heading, while definitions linked to supposition, hypothesis and logical argument – and the new insight that comes in step-by-step reasoning – relate to the intellectual function. For example, the suggestions offered at the opening of this chapter could be categorized as shown below.

An example of the framework of imaginative function, with participant responses inserted

SENSORY

'Thinking of things in their absence'
'Recalling the past'
'Pictures behind the eyes'
'Dreaming with all your senses on red alert'

INTUITIVE

'Dreaming of possibilities'
'Daydreaming'
'Seeing something as something else'
'Playful cognitive escapism'
'Seeing beyond the normal limitations'
'Imagination – thought unbounded'
'Seeing new connections between things'

AFFECTIVE

'Putting yourself in someone else's shoes'
'Creating in the mind experiences we've never had'
'Seeing from another point of view'
'The ability to act a part'

INTELLECTUAL

'Seeing what could be instead of what is'
'Bringing life to a different reality from the one present'
'Exploring the question "If this, then what?"'
'Creating the idea of an alternative reality'
'Thought about what *could* be'
'Playing with mental Lego'
'Creating new ideas about a product or task'

Seeking to stand in the students' shoes, the teacher may note that resistance to imagination can be rooted less in theological objections and more in earlier negative educational experiences. Douglas Purnell recounts his own fear of saying the wrong thing in preaching, which hindered his imaginative freedom. He traces the root of this anxiety to an incident he had at the age of 12, when he had written a story he thought was a wonderfully creative piece. Failing to grasp his authorial intention and without discussing the piece individually with the young Purnell, the teacher read out his work to the class as an example of poor writing, leading to his humiliation and a subsequent difficulty in trusting his imagination. He comments that 'many adult learners can tell similar stories', pointing up the need for theological colleges to 'become communities of healing in which people are encouraged to trust and express the work of their imagination'.[19] Adult learners who were schooled in a culture of standard assessment tests may not have had much opportunity for developing the free play of imagination, or for valuing imagination. A vital issue here is respecting the

---

19 Purnell, '"Educating the Whole Body"', pp. 222–3.

experiences – positive and negative – that students bring with them to the homiletics classroom.

Some students may be impatient with the stress on developing imagination as a spiritual discipline, because the pressure of upcoming preaching appointments, alongside the many other demands of theological training, leads to a desire to learn 'how to preach' in a more instrumental fashion. However, this impatience to learn the nuts and bolts of preaching as quickly as possible is usually rooted in a deep anxiety, which can be eased through imaginative engagement with God, out of which flows the confidence to preach. While equipping the preacher with appropriate skills is of great importance, the teacher should resist any sense that there is *a* right way to preach – this will hinder preachers from discovering their own preaching voice. The metaphor of a preaching toolbox is really helpful here – the learner being encouraged to gather methods and materials and decide how best to use and apply them as they discover, express and explore their own preaching styles. The contents of the preaching toolbox will develop over time if the preacher is actively seeking to engage their imagination: learning from experience (which includes the experience of so-called failure); theological engagement with Scripture and contextual issues; congregational feedback and learning from other preachers.

Inhabiting an imaginative pedagogy of homiletics means drawing from a wide range of resources to model imaginative engagement and to stimulate and equip the student preacher, both in terms of their theoretical grasp of homiletics and their practical engagement with preaching. As discussed in Chapter 5, the ways we imagine the preaching role have powerful theological entailments. Considerable experience of teaching preaching classes and running conferences on preaching have made it clear to me that many preachers simply have not considered their theology of preaching or their master metaphors. Weak theological foundations hamper deep reflective practice. Inviting students to explore the strengths and weaknesses of a range of similes for the preacher's role – preacher as teacher, herald, artist, spiritual director, jazz musician and jester – and develop their own models can creatively and playfully help to explore these issues.

In encouraging students to engage imaginatively with the biblical text, the homiletics tutor can also borrow from the techniques of the drama workshop. Such exercises invite a playful engagement with material that can break the strait-jacket of right/wrong thinking that often impedes learning. Careful exegetical work on a text can be followed up with hot-seating a character as a way of building an imaginatively affective connection, bringing the feelings and experiences of the biblical character closer to our own. Hot-seating enables the students to focus on and articulate the questions they bring to the text while also highlighting the question of what congregants might be asking about a text. Freeze-framing can be used to help students to consider the embodied nature of communication. For example, students might be asked to choose a biblical character involved in a particularly dramatic situation – for example, Peter after he had denied Christ and fled the scene; the elderly woman healed of her crippling back problem; Mary at the Annunciation; Paul on the Damascus road.[20] They are then instructed to freeze-frame a position and facial expression that communicate the emotions of their chosen character. The other participants are asked to see if they can draw inferences from the bodily communication and try to guess who is being represented. Exercises like this encourage students to consider how they use their bodies to add communicative force to their preaching.

The use of dramatic monologue can help students to engage in careful exegesis that is then used to make inferences about the character's perspectives, using that to write and present a dramatic monologue. Such a task requires the use of the affective imagination – exegetical skill in using biblical material and drawing apposite inferences from it and effective performance in terms of gesture, facial expression and use of space, vocal

---

20 Matt. 26.69–75; Mark 14.66–72; Luke 22.54–62; John 18.15–17, 25–27; Luke 13.10–17; Luke 1.26–38; Acts 9.1–5.

intonation and pace. Such exercises can develop imaginative muscle and homiletic confidence.

As we saw in Chapter 3, writing for the ear involves using lyrical language that is richly evocative. Student preachers need to be exposed to the power of poetic language and given opportunities to play with figurative language, identifying and discussing the effective use of the lyrical voice in sermons. This can be achieved in a wide variety of ways, such as:

- listening to and analysing religious radio reflections on local and national stations, critically reflecting on the effectiveness of the contributors' attempts to write for the ear;
- writing their own radio reflections and discussing these in groups, seeking outlets through local radio;
- analysing the sermons of effective lyrical preachers;
- thinking critically about their own use of language and the reasons why they have employed particular strategies.

An important aim in the teaching of preaching is to encourage preachers to be imaginatively reflective about all the dimensions of their craft and to help them connect with the imaginations of their hearers in the preaching event.

Igniting the Heart –
Concluding Thoughts

This book has aimed to establish the vital importance of the imagination in the contemporary preaching event. The contention throughout has been that the sermon is an essential part of the formation and worship of the Church. However, there is no room for preaching that is dull, pointless or irrelevant, if indeed there ever was. Sermons need to ignite the heart. Excellent monologue preaching can do this, the kind of preaching in which the hearers lean in to hear more, preaching that lifts vision to a greater apprehension of the reality of God and sounds out the call to live lives based on that reality. Such preaching sparks connections in the hearer, who weaves from these connections the sermon they need to hear in the given moment. Such preaching is utterly dependent on the Spirit of God brooding over the chaos and vulnerability of the preparation process, bringing to birth a new thing in the event of the sermon.

Imagination is vital to preaching if the hearts of the hearers are to ignite as people wake up to the reality of divine love pulsing through creation, concentrated in Christ and flowing out through the revelatory impulse of the Spirit. Imagination is an agent of divine transformation: it enables intuitive connection, sparks new vision, paints alternative vistas of hope-filled possibility and opens us to the perspective of the other. It shapes our ability to describe, to image and intimate. It governs the way we look upon others, ourselves and even the preaching role itself. Grasped by the Spirit, imagination clears the vision of the sinner, it causes the heart to catch and reorientates the will towards the worship of God.

As such it is vital to preaching.

Appendix

Sermon 1 – John 11.38–44

Imagine there is a jail cell, just here

There is a person inside the cell. Someone comes along and unlocks the door of the cell, and all the other doors of the compound. There is nothing to stop the person getting up and leaving. But they don't move.

Here's the question: Is the person free?

Well, yes – and no.

Yes – in the biggest sense of the word – there is nothing to prevent them leaving, and no – in the practical sense – because they remain in the prison.

Free and bound at the same time.

Hold that thought.

Let's jump right into the climactic moment of John 11

The crowd gather around Lazarus' tomb, jostling and jockeying for pole position.

Hear the mixed murmurings of compassion, anxiety and disapproval.

The babble of the bewildered.

Jesus frowns, greatly disturbed.

At his command, and in spite of Martha's horrified objection about the stench of death, they heave the stone aside.

Some recoil, aghast.

Some crane forward, intrigued.

Horror and hope displayed on the faces.

Jesus' voice cuts through the air.

He prays, calling on God, 'that [the crowd] may believe that you sent me'.

Silence.

[hold pause]

Then the cry:

   'Lazarus, come out . . .'

Some strain forward into the open mouth of the tomb.

What do they see?

Shuffling awkwardly, 'The dead man came out, his hands and feet bound with strips of cloth, and his face wrapped in a cloth.'

What do you see?

My imagination whirrs and jams – and presents me with something akin to Hammer meets Houdini. Not helpful.

Jesus' next words: *'Unbind him, and let him go.'*

   'Lazarus, come out . . .'

   'Unbind him, and let him go.'

Let me ask you a question:

'Why did Jesus go to the cross? Why did he die there?'

(Take responses. Almost certainly 'freedom' will be a word mentioned.)

   To connect us with the love of God.

   To free us from a debt we cannot pay.

   To free us from the devil's grip.

   To give us an example and set us free to love after that pattern.

   Take your pick of atonement theories; all are in some way about freedom . . .

Jesus comes to set us free

And yet . . . Consider the Church.

   How free is it? Free and bound at the same time? Perhaps?

Look, I know the teaching:

'If the spirit of God sets you free, you shall be free indeed.'

   'I came that they might have life in all its fullness.'

'The truth will make you free.'

I know the teaching. I know the theology. I believe it.

And yet . . . there is perhaps too easy a rhetoric of freedom, too simple a move from the tomb to the light of life and freedom. In so many ways, the Church (that's us) is bound up in the trappings of death.

I picture a figure emerging from the tomb bound in death's clothing, I recognize the halting shuffling, I hear it in the stories of others, I know it in myself. Perhaps it's familiar to you:

That person is free, gloriously free and yet not experiencing it fully.

Limited by the shrouds of contempt for another.

Blinded by prejudice.

Bound by the bonds of addiction.

Hamstrung by secret fantasies.

Hobbled by grasping avarice.

Perhaps we see it around us – this freedom/not freedom. The apparently successful minister exposed as an adulterer, seen face down at the end of a coke line, shown to be a con artist. It's like they came out of the tomb, but kept the death clothes on.

And how many of us, like Lazarus, heard the voice of Jesus calling us out of the tomb of deathly existence and into new life?

'Come out!'

Only then to find that the promised freedom is not yet reached.

We still need to be unbound and let go – we need to allow others to come close and help unwind death's couture.

'Unbind him and let him go.'

'Lazarus, come out . . .'

'Unbind him, and let him go.'

What's the distance between these two phrases? For many of us – it's a distance to be measured in years and not paces.

I picture a figure coming out of the tomb towards Christ, responding to the command to come out. They stumble towards him.

'Unbind her, and let her go.'

The response:

'*Actually, it's OK. I'll just put on a trackie over the clothes, don't want to be a burden, really it's fine. I'll sort it later.*'

Perhaps she is ashamed of the death clothes. They smell. They are stained. 'I'll keep them hidden, if it's all the same to you.'

How many of us in the Church are wearing death cloths under our clothing, hoping no one will notice that our step is limited and our freedom is not complete?

See again that prison – all the doors open and the figure remains inside.

Um . . . Is it possible to be free and yet not free?

Yes.

Is it possible to be free, free in actual fact, and yet practically shackled?

We know it is. We experience it. We see it.

'*Unbind him, and let him go*' – Do you notice how Jesus does not unbind Lazarus' death clothes? He calls the community to come and do this. This is a calling to the community around him to come and help unbind him.

Imagine if the community had said – '*Well, he's been oozing and secreting for four days into those cloths. I don't want to touch them, thanks. Make me unclean. He'll be OK. He's alive, stinks a bit, but we love him. Febreze him – he'll be fine.*'

As we come into land I want to make two clear points.

1 'Unbind them, and let them go.' In the place of Lazarus, we are called to submit to others as they unbind us. At the heart of all our journeying with God is to move from practical enslavement into the actual freedom he has given. When I find myself caught in unhelpful habits of mind and practice, what helps is when I tell a trusted friend and make myself accountable; when I submit to the hands that come to unbind me, I can shrug off the shackles of death. It's risky. It makes me vulnerable. I don't much like it. BUT if we are to experience the full freedom of Christ we need each other. Church is community, not a collection of individuals in silos.

2 Like the community surrounding Lazarus, we are called to
help each other get out of the grave clothes. At the heart
of all our journeying with God is to learn to help each
other get out of the grave clothes. Remember the line
from the song, 'Will you kiss the leper clean and do such
as this unseen' – easy to sing. We are called to actually do
it, to listen to people's stories: addiction to pornography,
booze, violence, work, unhealthy relationships, rage, resent-
ment, drug abuse, sexual abuse – all the stinking mess.
'Unbind them, and let them go.' That is Christ's command
to us.

Perhaps you identify with the image of Lazarus in a trackie –
with his grave clothes hidden underneath. Maybe now God is
calling you to ask for some help in unbinding the clothing of
death – so you can stride out in his freedom.

Perhaps you hear the call to get your hands dirty by touching
the dirty clothing of another's life, and God calls you tonight
to re-commit to that calling – to be an agent of bringing people
fully into freedom. Fully into the life and light Jesus has bought
and brought.

During communion, there will be opportunity to receive
anointing with oil – a sign of your openness to the spirit in
these matters.

There is also opportunity for prayer ministry – one way of
receiving help from others in the task of unbinding the shroud.
Amen.

Sermon 2 – Matthew 3.1–12

On the brink of the season of excess,
John the Baptist's voice
cuts through the growing aroma of
mulled wine and mince pies.
Never mind the Iceland and M&S ads –
John gives us winnowing forks and unquenchable fire.
Penitence. Judgement.
Provocative themes.
Challenging. Troubling. Scary.
John.

Last in the line of the Old Testament Prophets –
an edgy Elijah figure:
no rich fabrics,
no fine cuisine.
What kind of royalty does he herald
in his camel-hair robe?
This uncompromising locust-cruncher,
this wilderness wanderer.
His message insistent, uncompromising –
Baptizer John – bringer of heartburn.

Heart. Burn –
the searing awareness
of compromise and failure;
it's John who strikes the match.
Can you feel your heart strangely warmed?
'*Repent. Reconsider. Reorientate,*
for the kingdom of heaven has come near!
The Lord is on the move –
attend to the crooked pathways!
Straighten things out!'

Do you notice how they came to John?
Crowds of people

from Jerusalem and Judea and the Jordan region.
They came.
Why?
Some walked miles to hear a sermon.
Would we?

God-hungry they came.
Spirit-starved they came.
Looking and longing,
they came.

Two thousand years later,
have we lost our appetite?
Like children in a sweet shop,
has the Western Church
stuffed herself so full of self-indulgence
she has dulled her real hunger?

Listen to your stomach rumble.
Attend to your heartburn.
Baptizer John awakens us –
slothful sleepers –
to our deep desire for God.
A latent longing not met
in the potentially empty recitation
of our ritual confession.
Not to knock our liturgy,
but it has to be said that
the things of religion,
practised for themselves alone,
make us cold and dull and dangerous.

And along comes John –
railing against the viper brood;
those who come to him
to engage in outward religious practice,
with no inner change.

Seeking a talisman against the wrath of God.
Rugged individualism, dressed up as piety;
God help us.

John calls for a three-part
journey of repentance:
Sacramental – 'they were baptized by him'.
Verbal – 'they confessed their sins'.
Active – 'bear fruit worthy of repentance'.
We need all three elements
to guard against the lure of
empty, dangerous religion
that whitewashes the sepulchre
but fails to attend to the bones.

Listen to John in the cadences of our day.
'*So you've been a clergy woman.*
a professional religious –
And?
Wake up.
So you've been
a churchgoer all your life?
Big deal.
Is that your get-out-of-jail-free card
against the judgement day?
Wake up.
The genuineness of penitence is visible,
real, tangible, present, actual.
Will it be a laden apple tree,
boughs hanging heavy, rich with fruit –
or a twisted, stunted twig,
offering a few wizened wormy apples?'

John plays hardball.
No cheap grace.
Nothing soft in the axe of judgement
that comes with cutting truth.

I want to say to him:
'*Watch what you're doing with that axe.*
It's sharp. It's dangerous. It hurts.'

Perhaps we stand at a distance
from John the disturber,
listening and resisting,
attentive and appalled,
desiring and despairing?

After all,
we know ourselves.
We know our petty failure:
pitiful cycles of small-mindedness,
the gritty chaff of selfishness that
stops us seeing right.
Blinkered blindness binds us
from meeting neighbour-need.
We know our tendency to grumble and grouse,
judging others from our thrones self-righteousness.
Oh, we stamp our feet,
blast our horns –
slam the phone down –
short-fused, short-sighted, short on humour.

But John is just too full of God
to let us off.
The granite solid love of the Baptizer cries out:
'*Repent. Reconsider. Reorientate,*
for the kingdom of heaven has come near.
Attend to the crooked pathways.
Straighten things out.
Imagination, heart, mind –
washed and renewed.'

Perhaps we fear we are too lost,
hapless, hopeless sinners?

But stop.
Look at John's index finger.
See where he points,
never wavering,
beyond himself,
beyond his watery cleansing,
to the One whose shoes
he is not worthy to pick up.
To the One who burns away
the husk and rind of sin,
who baptizes in God's Spirit,
plunging us deep into the divine –
where the little, the lost,
the humble and hamstrung,
the foolish and frail
might be healed and freed.
Thank God.

Oh God,
take the chaff away.
Burn it up –
all that separates and divides,
all that makes us cold,
all that fuels the forge of war.
Burn up the hatred in our hearts.
Immolate our indifference.
Incinerate the enmity
between the nations.
Refiner's fire – save us.

Oh Jesus,
you see beyond the surfaces.
You hear the heartbeat.
You know us.
Forgive us.
Lead us in wisdom and understanding,
good counsel and holy might.

Teach us loving fear,
worshipful awe,
the art of Holy friendship
with you.

Spirit of the Living God,
draw us into the world
of which Isaiah speaks:
may water flow in the world's wildernesses;
in the arid hopelessness of hatred.
May the burning sand of alienation
be cooled with springs of living water.
Where our hearts are dry and dusty,
bring new life.
May our hearts blossom abundantly.

Holy God – three in one and one in three –
we long for that day when sorrow and sighing
shall flee away.
May we find a way through the desert places
walking upon your holy highway.

Help us to hope for, work for, pray for
a time when knowledge of you will
flood creation,
saturate and soak the nations.
A time when the snake-like sting of death
that diseases our spirits
and corrupts our flesh
will be no more.
When the groans of creation
will be ended.
Show us how
to work for that day,
to bring love and hope,
forgiveness and resources
into the lives of our neighbours.

We can do so little without you.
Grant us an Advent
of honesty and hope.
Embrace our hearts
with your holed and Holy hands.

Amen.

Sermon 3 – John 20.1–18

I love this passage from John's Gospel, pacy, full of emotion, bursting with question, the camera cutting back and forth, characters running here and there. It is the experience of Mary that carries us through this passage. She is the consistent character throughout, and as we sit on her shoulder as the reader, we can observe the movements of her conversion: Through unbelief, to experience and realization. **Unbelief. Experience. Realization.** The stages of conversion.

It's difficult for many of us, but try and imagine you had never heard John's account of the resurrection before.

'Early on the first day of the week, while it was still dark . . .'

The clues are all there.

The first day of the week.

The first day of something new: at this stage neither Mary, nor the uninitiated hearer, realizes just how transformative, cataclysmic and wonderful that something new will be.

'While it was still dark, Mary Magdalene went to the tomb.'

'While it as still dark' – the language points us towards the gloom of Mary's grief and lack of understanding.

Let's try and home in on her point of view:

She has witnessed the horrific death of a man to whom she was devoted.

She was there at the foot of the cross.

She was there when the spear was jabbed into his side.

She was there when the blood and water poured out.

She was there as his mother and the other women wept.

I imagine she watched as the body was taken down, wrapped in cloths and sealed up in the garden tomb.

What did she feel as the stone was rolled into place?

Can you imagine?

Have you heard the sound of earth falling on a coffin lid?

If you have, really heard it, then you have some insight into Mary's darkness.

It is a terrible darkness.

It is the darkness that snuffs out hope, a suffocating creeping darkness that erodes any belief in a future.

It is the poisonous, insinuating darkness of death.

It's bleak.

And yet . . .

And yet . . .

There is a competition going on in the first line of this passage.

'Early on the first day of the week, while it was still dark . . .'

Darkness dominates, yes, but we know that dawn is coming – a thought worth clinging to in those times when we wrestle with depression, illness, grief and struggle.

Yes – darkness might surround us now – but with God, dawn from on high will break upon us.

It always comes, following even the wildest, blackest nights.

Yes – the night hours are long, but nothing can stop daybreak.

Here in John 20 verse 1 we have the Christian hope encapsulated in the image of the early morning darkness.

The darkness must fade.

But at this early stage, Mary is blinded by the darkness of unbelief.

She grasps at the most natural human explanation to explain the stone rolled away and the empty tomb – grave robbery.

Put yourself in her shoes.

You take flowers to the grave of a loved one and the grave is open, empty. What emotions would you feel? Shock, horror, anger, compounded loss, panic? So she dashes off for help and Peter and the beloved disciple run to see what's happened.

The story is full of edginess, urgency, confusion – and masterful detail. The disciple Jesus loved arrives first, bends over, looks in the tomb, sees the strips of linen, doesn't go in. Why not? Why is he hesitant? Fear of pollution? Fear of death? Simple shock?

Then Peter, bold, reckless Peter, arrives and dives right into the tomb, taking in the details of the strips of linen, and the burial cloth used to wrap Jesus' head, folded separately. Look at the detail.

The camera focuses right in on these empty grave clothes, and the uninitiated reader, along with Mary, Peter and the beloved disciple, can only gaze and wonder. Grave clothes, but no body? What on earth has happened here?

Finally, the other disciple enters the tomb, sees and believes. What he actually believes we are not told. We are told that 'they didn't understand from Scripture that Jesus had to rise from the dead'. Who are *they*? Simon Peter and Mary? All three of them? Whatever, it seems to me that it is perfectly possible to believe without understanding. The beloved disciple is in that place of gradual awakening, the grey light of dawning realization, the place of knowing that something massively significant has happened, without being able to articulate it. He is moving from **unbelief** to **experience**.

And so what? How do you understand the process of coming to faith? This part of the story – the arrival of the men, their different approaches to the situation, the different reactions – should remind us that conversion through those stages of **unbelief, experience, realization** is a unique process for each of us, a process intimately connected to our character and disposition. Faith cannot be forced. It is more than an intellectual process. It is a journey – through darkness to light. For some the light dawns more quickly than for others, and many are content to whistle in the dark.

Patience is a watchword for mission.

Meanwhile, back in the story, Mary's journey is about to take another turn.

The narrative shifts and the two men depart, going back to their homes, leaving Mary weeping.

A solitary woman weeping by a grave.

Again, step into her shoes:

The men she ran to for help have left her, gone home, but where is her home? Jesus' death has left her dislocated, miserable and alone – even reaching out to others has failed. She is locked in the isolation of her grief.

We must appreciate this if we are to experience with her something of the transformative wonder to come, when hope takes the place of despair.

The story moves up a gear with the reference to two angels who question Mary. Look how casually they are introduced into what has been, up until now, a human story. They are just dropped in, served up by the Gospel writer as though dishing out something very ordinary. Two angels in white – seated where his body had been, one at the head, one at the feet. The two disciples saw the vestiges of death, the grave clothes. Mary is on the way to seeing the fullness of life, and angels are a signpost for the reader that a naturalistic understanding of what has happened – that is, the body's been stolen – simply won't do. More is afoot than simple grave robbery.

There is no sense that Mary recognizes the two men as angelic beings. The writer tells us that they are, but Mary shows no recognition of their status. She is still struggling to hold on to a natural explanation, 'They have taken my Lord away and I don't know where they have put him'.

She is still in the darkness of **unbelief**. Jesus, in her mind, is dead. Events are being fitted into a pre-existent framework of very reasonable assumptions. She watched him die. Presumably she was there when the tomb was sealed. The only logical explanation is that someone stole the body. But God is not bound by human logic. In his kingdom all is turned on its head, the last become the first, the outcast becomes the wedding guest and the dead will become the living. God is not bound by human assumption. But for Mary, still in the darkness, this realization has yet to dawn.

When she turns and sees Jesus standing behind her, she fits this into her pre-existent framework of assumptions. It's a garden; he must be a gardener.

How often do we miss seeing God at work because of our assumptions?

There is a delicious irony about this case of mistaken identity, given the many biblical references to God as the gardener.

'You're right, Mary, when you think he's a gardener; you just don't yet know how right you are.'

For the third time in this story, Mary articulates the heart of her problem: her Lord has been taken away and she doesn't know where he is.

The pantomime audience in me wants to cry out, 'He's in front of you!'

Still Mary is in the darkness of **unbelief**. For her, the stages of **experience** and **realization** come all at once. There is no gradual dawning of realization. For her, the morning sun bursts out from the clouds in one dramatic moment.

'Mary,' he names her, and 'she turns towards him.'

'Rabboni!' She has experienced a radical shift of perspective. Her mourning is turned into dancing.

Experience and **realization** collide, and everything, everything has changed.

The light of understanding floods through her and she tries to touch him, hold him, connect physically.

Jesus' injunction that she shouldn't hold on to him serves as a reminder of the mystery and wonder of the resurrection.

Now is not the time for her to hold him, now is the time for her to go and tell the others. So Mary, the first Apostle, takes the good news to the disciples.

The movement from **unbelief** to **experience** and then **realization** is different for different people. There is no one model, no one-size-fits-all. Mission and pastoral care need to take careful note of this.

In terms of the spiritual journey, I wonder if actually this three-staged process might be better represented as a spiral, rather than a line.

That movement of conversion – from **unbelief, through experience** to **realization** – is a movement we are constantly engaged in, through prayer and worship, moving more deeply in all aspects of our lives into encounter with the Risen Lord.

If we are working on the model of a three-stage, linear process, full stop, we run the danger of thinking we have arrived at belief and that's it, but Jesus calls into deeper stages of belief, of realization of who he is, how much he loves us and what his resurrection means for us and for the world.

Unbelief, experience, realization. This is a story that begs us to look again at where we are in relation to the resurrection, to meditate on it, to reflect on it, but more than anything, to take hope in it.

For it is the source of all our hope.

Amen.

Sermon 4 – Luke 8.22–39

Initially, as I reflected on our Gospel passage, a sermon began to take shape that linked the calming of the storm on the lake and the calming of the storm-tossed soul of Legion, with a nod to verses in Psalm 65, which speak of God 'silencing the roaring of the seas and answering us with deliverance'. The application would then have been something along the lines of trusting Jesus – the one who brings calm into chaos. Sermon written, job done. [*dust hands*] On to the next thing.

But as this sermon was born, another sermon emerged, gripping its heel, and usurping it.

An uncomfortable sermon.

A sermon that kept asking me to shift the focus – away from the theme of calm, to the storm that Jesus himself creates.

Result? A less comfortable address . . .

Jesus the storm bringer

First let's zoom in on the disciples after the storm has been stilled. [*use eye line, gesture and hand movement to indicate the disciples' position in the body of the preaching space*]

There they are, hair plastered down by lake water, crouching in a half-submerged boat, its hull caressed by gentle wavelets. For all the calm around them, in their hearts and minds they are buffeted by questions: fear, awe, wonder. Perhaps a tempest of recrimination blasts at them? They have woken up to their spiritual amnesia.

Peter – had you forgotten so soon? [*looking towards the imagined Peter*]

You saw the nets breaking as the fish slapped into the boat.

You recognized Jesus as Holy, as Lord.

You saw him heal people. You heard him teach.

You were there at Nain when he told the dead man to get up, and he did.

[*turn from Peter to congregation*] No, I don't think the calm on the lake is matched by calm in the disciples' hearts:

[for each question/statement, alter head movement to repre-
sent a different speaking voice]

'How could we have been so stupid?'

'How could we have forgotten?'

'Where is our faith?'

'He stands before us – he has power over the elements.'

'Here is God with us.'

Jesus the storm bringer

[turn from disciples to congregation]

And what of us? Are we immune to this spiritual amnesia?

Have you had those moments of an intense sense of God, times when you have prayed and seen God at work?

That mountaintop view that overwhelmed you with awe?

That catchy refrain in a song that spoke straight into your situation?

Sitting in the sublime beauty of a quiet cathedral, infused with a sense of presence?

A moment with a mentor or friend when you suddenly saw that what looked like death is a gateway to life?

Perhaps you write your experience in a journal and come across it sometime later and you are surprised by the memory.

'How could I have forgotten this?'

The tensions, trivialities, and traumas of life have robbed you.

The banality of life numbed you in its routine.

Spiritual amnesia.

It shrinks Jesus down until he is dashboard-sized.

[use forefinger and thumb to indicate this shrinkage]

We forget – the Lord of heaven and earth,

God almighty, *[looking up, big gesture]* is only a heartbeat away. *[gesture coming in close]*

Where is our faith?

Sometimes we need a storm to wake us up.

Jesus is a storm bringer

He brings a tempest of realization that tears up our self-reliance, uproots our pint-sized idols – 'Who then is this, that he commands even the winds and the water, and they obey him?' Who is this and what will following him mean? All our old ways of living and being are rearranged, reordered around him. What will this mean? What will it cost? Where will this take us? 'They were afraid and amazed.'

What of us?

Let's look now at that second story.

Legion the storm-tossed man who has roared and raged in the place of death, disturbed and disturbing. The locals must have known all about him; he was once a man of the city. But now . . .

A frightening case. The tomb man. Outcast. Unmanageable. Some family's shame. '*Oh, we don't speak about uncle Enoch.*'

Jesus encounters him, and when the people come to see what's happened, there he is, 'sitting at the feet of Jesus, clothed and in his right mind'.

The tempests of rage that blasted him out into the wilds are no more.

The waves of madness that robbed him of dignity are stilled.

The Legion of demons has gone.

So we might think all is well – storm stilled, all calm. Job done.

But no . . .

Jesus is a bringer of storms

A tempest is gathering in the wake of his actions. The Gerasene people are in turmoil. The tip of their tornado points down, not at the man but at the pigs.

Mark's Gospel tells us there are 2,000 of them. That's a massive herd. That's maybe 400,000 pounds of meat. That's a major business investment. That's primary income. That's employment. That's financial well-being.

And it's just gone over a cliff.
And for what?
For some insane guy who hangs out at the local cemetery.

Jesus is a bringer of storms

Luke tells us that the people were 'seized with great fear'. Jesus has come into their territory.

A Jew – but he is not perturbed by being on Gentile turf, with pigs around, facing a demonic man who is naked and in the place of death. Jesus comes into the place of uncleanliness, because that man matters. The people push Jesus away because he implicitly asks them to rethink what is important. They are left with a choice. Will they engage with Jesus, embrace the once mad man into their community, work together to survive the damage to their local industry, hear what this powerful healer has to teach them, find out who he is, reorientate their lives around him?

No chance. It's all too much.

Too frightening.

This man Jesus is powerful and dangerous.

He brings change.

Their set ways are challenged.

Our calm existence is disturbed.

Deeply disturbed.

Understandably, they ask him to leave – and he respects this.

But graciously, Jesus leaves a bit of storm behind, to disturb their calm.

He commands the man to go back to his home and declare how much God has done for him.

This man will be the one to create waves in their cosy world – his very existence a living sign that their horizons are limited; he is a storm cloud in the blue azure of their deluded outlook.

An outlook that says the pigs mattered more than the man.

An outlook that brooked not one word of celebration.

Not a hint of thanksgiving.

Not a suggestion of welcome.

Not an iota of joy.

Not a whiff of excitement.
Only fear.

Jesus is a storm bringer
His power uproots expectations and challenges convictions.

But it seems to me that if we are in that storm we have a choice. We can either tell him to push off far from our shores, or we can ask him to dwell with us, helping us to endure the storm that demands a change of heart, mind, perspective.

Perhaps we have cosied up to a comfortable outlook, with a pint-sized Jesus we can manipulate at will?

Perhaps we have allowed spiritual amnesia to rob us of the awe that once filled our experience of God?

Perhaps we ended up in a place where our calm and well-being matters more than the white-lightning drinker in the cemetery.

Perhaps we have settled for a superficial calm that allows us to bury our meanness, lack of love, lack of forgiveness, our addictions and peccadilloes.

Jesus is a storm bringer – bringing healing to our amnesia, bringing challenge to our perspective, to who and what we value.

Have we the wisdom to pray for a storm and for the faith to ride it out with Christ?

Perhaps we lack courage – but it's worth remembering that a calm life can be boring, dull, predictable and empty, and storms can be exciting, wild, energizing, invigorating and transforming.

Jesus – cook up a storm and lead us on.
Amen.

Sermon 5 – Ezekiel 37

The book of Ezekiel. Weird and wonderful.

Let's jump in the time machine, spin the dial and take a journey back in time.

The year is 596 BC, or thereabouts.

Ezekiel, writer of our Old Testament passage, finds himself caught up in a deportation. God's people are being taken to Babylon.

Taken far from home to a strange land. Far from Jerusalem. Far from the Temple. Far from all that is familiar and secure. And it must seem they are far, far, far from God.

Fast-forward five years into this exilic experience and God calls Ezekiel in a strange and marvellous vision – you can read about that in chapter 1.

In the second chapter, God commissions Ezekiel as a prophet to his impudent, stubborn and rebellious people.

So in exile Ezekiel prophesies, enacting all kinds of strange things that represent God's judgement against his people. If a picture is worth a thousand words, then Ezekiel is pretty verbose. His prophecy is a gallery of word pictures and mini-dramas.

The first section of Ezekiel's ministry is chock-full of God's judgements against his people for their wilful disobedience. It makes uncomfortable reading indeed. But in time judgement is replaced by the theme of restoration (which starts at chapter 36). The people have betrayed God, they deserve nothing, but God acts in accordance with his great name and resolves to restore them, to shepherd them, that the nations might see and know that God has acted and that his own people might recognize, mourn and repent of their ways.

So that's the whistle-stop background.

We have arrived in Ezekiel chapter 37.

Time to disembark our time machine. Everybody off.

We step out into an eerie scene – hot and quiet. Still, deathly still.

On the bleached white sea on which you stand you pick out skulls, tibias, fibulas, jaw bones, tarsals, metatarsals, ribs, spines, ulnas, phalanges, you spot the odd kneecap here and there.

Bleached bones, many in number.

A catastrophe has occurred. The dead are dishonoured.

They have had no burial, but have been picked clean by scavengers.

Bones. Bones. Bones.

Bones under your feet.

Bones as far as your eye can see.

Bones crunching underfoot.

This is death valley.

I don't know about you, but I don't like it here.

So what does death valley symbolize?

The bones represent the whole house of Israel.

As a people in exile they are dead men and women, there is no future for the exiles.

They say '*Our bones are dried up and our hope is lost, we are cut off, completely.*' They have lost their homeland, their homes.

They are separated from the Temple, from Jerusalem – both of which will soon be utterly destroyed.

Far from all that is familiar and secure.

It must seem they are far, far, far from God.

Ezekiel is literally and metaphorically preaching to the dead.

Can you hear the words of Psalm 137, playing in the background?

'*By the rivers of Babylon, where we sat down, there we wept, as we remembered Zion . . .*

How can we sing the LORD's song in a strange land?'

This is the soundtrack to our scene.

Standing amid this sea of bleached dry bones, faced with the question, '*Mortal, can these bones live,*' we might be tempted to say: '*Not a chance. Are you mad? They are bones!*'

Really, the situation is utterly hopeless. Quite beyond help.

But God . . .

But with God nothing is ever utterly hopeless.

But God . . . God can do a new thing – even in situations of apparent futility.

God commands Ezekiel to speak to the bones, to speak into the place of death.

God includes Ezekiel as his agent in his new work.

God uses people, works with people to bring the message of life, even though only divine initiative can transform the death of exile.

Only God can redeem and restore.

Ezekiel prophesies, and our eerie scene is transformed into one that is bizarre, wonderful, even comical.

'*Suddenly there was a noise, a rattling, and the bones came together, bone to its bone.*'

Skulls seeking jawbones, tibias linking with fibulas, tarsals marrying metatarsals, ribs and spines, hips and femurs rattling about, kneecaps flying through the air.

Click, clack, rattle – bones are on the move.

This is wild – a dance of fusion in the valley of death.

Then, not for the squeamish, the vision of sinews and flesh and skin all growing back. Decomposition, decay and death are reversed.

So now death valley is peopled with lifeless bodies.

Again Ezekiel is asked to prophesy over the bodies of those slain. In God's name, he calls the breath of God, the *ruach* of God, to come upon these slain, and they stand, a vast living, breathing, multitude.

God reverses decomposition and death.

God brings life to the lifeless place.

Utter hopelessness now bursts with new possibilities.

From death valley a new thing is birthed.

Imagine you are in exile – you hear Ezekiel's prophecy of restoration.

Do you mock him – or do you dare to hope?

Then (verse 12) the metaphor in this prophecy of restoration changes.

We are no longer in the valley of dry bones; now we stand in a graveyard and God is imaged as a tomb raider, who promises to open up his people's graves and bring them up and back to the land of Israel.

He does this so they will know that he is the Lord, and they are his people.

Only God can reverse the irreversible, bringing exiles home.

Um . . .

Let's jump back in the time machine, spin the dial and come back here, Sunday, 5 May 2013, St Mary Magdalene Church, Belmont.

We get out, stretch our legs and wonder.

What do these strange experiences in death valley and the garden of graves say to us?

The million-dollar question is always, 'And so what?'

Like the people of Israel, who knew God but were stubborn and stupid, we can land ourselves in a heap of desolation by our hypocritical and contradictory behaviour.

Like them, so often we believe we put God first – but we have idols aplenty:

Children, family, status, work, money, image, freedom, comfort, well-being and myriad assorted addictions and peccadilloes that can usurp God's place in our lives.

So often we call ourselves God's people but we bitch and moan and put people down. I am drawing here from observation of myself – not pointing the finger. Sometimes we can put the boot in with the most civilized of language:

'*Bless her, she can't help it, but I heard . . .*'

'*Well, I like him well enough but . . .*'

If we are honest – we are often surrounded by the dry bones of our poor attitudes and failures. Our spiritual lives can be as deathly as that valley of dry bones.

But listen – with God the bones are rattling!

So often our selfish decisions, perhaps in buying cheap clothing, affect God's people elsewhere. We distance ourselves from this. We separate our behaviour from the suffering of others.

We don't care for the poor. Spiritually we can become split apart, fragmented and in bits.

But listen – with God the bones are rattling back to life!

Sometimes people wind up in exile, lost and alone, because of the behaviour of others. Poor examples, harsh words, abusive treatment, degradation, misery and we find ourselves sitting on a heap of bones in a dark place and it seems things are hopeless.

But listen – the breath of God is stirring the air.

This passage orientates us towards God's ultimate defeat of death in Jesus. Spiritually, emotionally, ethically, even physically – God calls and will call the exiles home.

After judgement comes hope. A hope based not on our merits – face it, we haven't, of ourselves, got any – but on the holy love of God, whose name will be upheld for ever.

So – be hopeful. Trust again.

God brings light from darkness.

The darkness we bring upon ourselves through stupid, selfish behaviour. The darkness others inflict on us thoughtlessly, or deliberately. The darkness we usher in when our words and actions turn off the light for another. The darkness of sickness. The darkness of depression and despair. The darkness of loneliness. The darkness of a world at war. The darkness of communities in which fear reigns. The darkness of the veil of sin. The darkness of death.

'Mortal, can these bones live?'

The Easter faith says 'YES'.

Then prophesy, mortals of Saint Mary Magdalene Church. Speak up.

In word and action – at home, in the gym, in the pub, at school, at the snooker club, at work, in the supermarket, on the street, in the church.

Speak of the Spirit of God who comes, and does new things, who acts that people might know who he is. That people might be filled with his Spirit. That all might come home from exile – to the Promised Land. Listen, the bones are rattling, as the Spirit brings us home. Home – to the heart of God.

Amen.

Bibliography

Astley, Jeff, *Ordinary Theology: Looking, Listening and Learning in Theology*, Aldershot: Ashgate, 2002.

Astley, Jeff, *Exploring God-talk: Using Language in Religion*, London: Darton, Longman & Todd, 2004.

Astley, Jeff, 'Giving Voice to the Ordinary', in *Exchanges of Grace: Essays in Honour of Ann Loades*, ed. Natalie K. Watson and Stephen Burns, London: SCM Press, 2008, pp. 204–7.

Augustine, *De Doctrina Christiana*, www.georgetown.edu/faculty/jod/augustine/ddc.html.

Austin, J. L., *How to do Things with Words*, Oxford: Clarendon Press, 1962.

Avis, Paul, *God and the Creative Imagination: Metaphor, Symbol and Myth in Religion and Theology*, London: Routledge, 1999.

Baillie, D. M., *The Theology of the Sacraments and Other Papers*, London: Faber & Faber, 1957.

Baker, John Austin, *The Foolishness of God*, London: Darton, Longman & Todd, 1970.

Barth, Karl, *The Word of God and the Word of Man*, trans. Douglas Horton, New York: Harper & Row, 1957.

Barth, Karl, *Prayer and Preaching*, trans. B. E. Hooke, London: SCM Press, 1964.

Barth, Karl, *Church Dogmatics* I/1, trans. G. T. Thomson, Edinburgh: T. & T. Clark, 1975.

Barth, Karl, *Homiletics*, trans. Geoffrey W. Bromley and Donald D. Daniels, Louisville, KY: John Knox Press, 1991.

Black, Max, *Models and Metaphors: Studies in Language and Philosophy*, New York: Cornell University Press, 1962.

Boff, Leonardo, *Sacraments of Life: Life of the Sacraments*, Washington, DC: Pastoral Press, 1987.

Booth, Wayne, 'Metaphor as Rhetoric: The Problem of Evaluation', *Critical Enquiry* 5:1 (1978), pp. 49–72.

Brann, Eva, *The World of the Imagination*, Savage, MD: Rowman & Littlefield, 1991.

Brown, David, *Tradition and Imagination: Revelation and Change*, Oxford: Oxford University Press, 1999.

Brown, David, *Discipleship and Imagination: Christian Tradition and Truth*, Oxford: Oxford University Press, 2000.

Brown, David, *God and the Enchantment of Place: Reclaiming Human Experience*, Oxford: Oxford University Press, 2006.

Brown, David, *God and Grace of Body: Sacrament in Ordinary*, Oxford: Oxford University Press, 2007.

Brown, David, *God and Mystery in Words: Experience through Metaphor and Drama*, Oxford: Oxford University Press, 2008.

Brown, David and Ann Loades (eds), *The Sense of the Sacramental: Movement and Measure in Art and Music, Place and Time*, London: SPCK, 1995.

Brown, David and Ann Loades (eds), *Christ: The Sacramental Word – Incarnation, Sacrament and Poetry*, London: SPCK, 1996.

Brown Taylor, Barbara, *The Preaching Life*, Norwich: Canterbury Press, 2014.

Bruce, Kate, Ben Blackwell and Peter Phillips, *The View from the Pew*, Durham: CODEC Publications, 2009.

Brueggemann, Walter, *Finally Comes the Poet: Daring Speech for Proclamation*, Minneapolis, MN: Fortress Press, 1989.

Buechner, Frederick, *Whistling in the Dark*, San Francisco: Harper, 1993.

Buttrick, David, 'Interpretation and Preaching', *Interpretation* 35 (1981), pp. 46–58.

Buttrick, David, *Homiletic Moves and Structures*, Philadelphia: Fortress Press, 1987.

Coggan, Donald, *On Preaching*, London: SPCK, 1978.

Coggan, Donald, *A New Day for Preaching: The Sacrament of the Word*, London: SPCK, 1996.

Cohen, David and Stephen A. MacKeith, *The Development of Imagination*, London and New York: Routledge, 1992.

Cox, Harvey, *The Feast of Fools: A Theological Essay on Festivity and Fantasy*, Cambridge, MA: Harvard University Press, 1969.

Dart, Lisa, 'Literacy and the Lost World of the Imagination', *Educational Research* 43:1 (2001), pp. 63–77.

Daston, Lorraine, 'Fear and Loathing of the Imagination in Science', *Daedalus* 127:1, Science in Culture (Winter 1998), pp. 73–95.

Dykstra, Craig, 'Pastoral and Ecclesial Imagination', in *The Life Abundant: Practical Theology, Theological Education, and Christian Ministry*, ed. Dorothy C. Bass and Craig Dykstra, Grand Rapids, MI: Eerdmans, 2008, pp. 41–61.

Eslinger, Richard L., *Pitfalls in Preaching*, Grand Rapids, MI: Eerdmans, 1996.

Farley, W. Edward, 'Can Preaching Be Taught?', *Theology Today* 62:2 (2005), pp. 171–80.

Florence, Anna Carter, 'The Preaching Imagination', in *Teaching Preaching as a Christian Practice*, ed. Thomas G. Long and Nora Tubbs Tisdale, Louisville, KY: Westminster John Knox Press, 2008, pp. 116–33.

Gadamer, Hans-Georg, *Truth and Method*, trans. Joel Weinsheimer and Donald G. Marsha, London: Continuum, 2004.

Greeley, Andrew, *The Catholic Imagination*, Berkeley and Los Angeles: University of California Press, 2000.

Green, Garrett, *Imagining God: Theology and the Religious Imagination*, Grand Rapids, MI: Eerdmans, 1989.

Guite, Malcolm, *Faith, Hope and Poetry: Theology and the Poetic Imagination*, Farnham: Ashgate, 2012.

Hajdu, David, 'Wynton's Blues', *The Atlantic Webzine*, 1 March 2003, www.unz.org/Pub/AtlanticWeb-2003mar-00025.

Hart, Trevor A., 'Imagining Evangelical Theology', in *Evangelical Futures: A Conversation on Evangelical Method*, ed. John G. Stackhouse Jr, Grand Rapids, MI: Baker Books, 2000, pp. 191–200.

Hart, Trevor A., 'Art, Performance and the Practice of Christian Faith', in *Faithful Performances: Enacting Christian Tradition*, ed. Trevor A. Hart and Steven R. Guthrie, Aldershot: Ashgate, 2007, pp. 1–9.

Hart, Trevor A., 'The Sense of an Ending: Finitude and the Authentic Performance of Life', in *Faithful Performances: Enacting Christian Tradition*, ed. Trevor A. Hart and Steven R. Guthrie, Aldershot: Ashgate, 2007, pp. 167–88.

Harris, Paul L., *The Work of the Imagination: Understanding Children's Worlds*, Oxford: Blackwell, 2000.

Heywood, David, *Transforming Preaching: The Sermon as a Channel for God's Word*, London: SPCK, 2013.

Hilkert, Mary Catherine, *Naming Grace: Preaching and the Sacramental Imagination*, New York: Continuum, 1997.

Huizinga, Johan, *Homo Ludens*, London: Paladin, 1970.

Janowiak, Paul, *The Holy Preaching: The Sacramentality of the Word in the Liturgical Assembly*, Collegeville, MN: Liturgical Press, 2000.

Johnson, Mark, *The Body in the Mind: The Bodily Basis of Meaning, Imagination, and Reason*, Chicago: University of Chicago Press, 1987.

Jones, Kirk Byron, *The Jazz of Preaching: How to Preach with Great Freedom and Joy*, Nashville, TN: Abingdon Press, 2004.

Kaufman, Gordon D., *The Theological Imagination: Constructing the Concept of God*, Philadelphia: The Westminster Press, 1981.

Knights, L. C., *Some Shakespearian Themes*, London: Chatto & Windus, 1959.

Kuhn, Thomas S., *The Structure of Scientific Revolutions*, 3rd edn, Chicago: University of Chicago Press, 1996.

Lakoff, George and Mark Johnson, *Metaphors We Live By*, Chicago: University of Chicago Press, 1980.

Lakoff, George and Mark Turner, *More than Cool Reason: A Field Guide to Poetic Metaphor*, London: University of Chicago Press, 1989.

Lee, Harper, *To Kill a Mockingbird*, London: Heinemann, 1960.

Le Guin, Ursula K., 'Bryn Mawr Commencement Address', in *Dancing at the Edge of the World: Thoughts on Words, Women, Places*, New York: Grove Press, 1989, pp. 147–60.

Levy, Sandra M., *Imagination and the Journey of Faith*, Cambridge, MA: Eerdmans, 2008.

Liu, Eric and Scott Noppe-Brandon, *Imagination First: Unlocking the Power of Possibility*, San Francisco: Wiley, 2009.

Loades, Ann, 'The Sacramental, a New Sense', in *The Gestures of God*, ed. Geoffrey Rowell, London: Continuum, 2004, pp. 161–72.

Locke, John, *Essay Concerning Human Understanding*, Oxford: Clarendon Press, 1894.

MacDonald, George, 'The Imagination: Its Function and its Culture' (1867), www.wordiq.com/books/Dish_Of_Orts,_A_:_Chiefly_Papers_On_The_Imagination,_And_On_Shakespeare.

Macquarrie, John, *A Guide to the Sacraments*, London: SCM Press, 1997.

McClure, John S., *The Roundtable Pulpit: Where Leadership and Preaching Meet*, Nashville, TN: Abingdon, 1995.

McFague, Sallie, *Metaphorical Theology: Models of God in Religious Language*, Philadelphia: Fortress Press, 1982.

McFague, Sallie, *Speaking in Parables: A Study in Metaphor and Theology*, 2nd edn, London: SCM Press, 2002.

McIntyre, John, *Faith, Theology and Imagination*, Edinburgh: Handsel Press, 1987.

McKim, Robert H., *Experiences in Visual Thinking*, Belmont, CA: Wadsworth, 1972.

Miles, Margaret, *Image as Insight*, Boston, MA: Beacon Press, 1961.

Mitchell, Jolyon, *Visually Speaking: Radio and the Renaissance of Preaching*, Edinburgh: T. & T. Clark, 1999.

Moltmann, Jürgen, *The Crucified God*, London: SCM Press, 1984.

Nieman, James R., 'Preaching that Drives People from the Church', in *A Reader on Preaching: Making Connections*, ed. David Day, Jeff Astley and Leslie J. Francis, Aldershot: Ashgate, 2005, pp. 247–54.

Norrington, David C., *To Preach or Not to Preach: The Church's Urgent Question*, Carlisle: Paternoster Press, 1996.

Northcutt, Kay L., *Kindling Desire for God: Preaching as Spiritual Direction*, Minneapolis, MN: Fortress Press, 2009.

O'Leary, Donal, 'Imagination: The Forgotten Dimension', *The Furrow* 57:10 (2006), pp. 519–27.

Osborne, Kenan B., *Christian Sacraments in a Postmodern World: A Theology for the Third Millennium*, New York: Paulist Press, 1999.

Pagitt, Doug, *Preaching Re-imagined: The Role of the Sermon in Communities of Faith*, Grand Rapids, MI: Zondervan, 2005.

Purnell, Douglas, '"Educating the Whole Body": Addressing and Equipping the Imagination in Theological Education', *Pastoral Psychology* 49:3 (2001), pp. 205–25.

Rahner, Karl, 'Priest and Poet', in *Theological Investigations Vol. 3, Theology of the Spiritual Life*, London: Darton, Longman & Todd, 1967, pp. 294–317.

Ramsey, Ian T., *Religious Language*, London: SCM Press, 1957.

Ramsey, Ian T. (ed.), *Words About God*, London: SCM Press, 1971.

Richards, I. A., *Philosophy of Rhetoric*, New York: Oxford University Press, 1965.

Riegert, Edward, *Imaginative Shock: Preaching and Metaphor*, Burlington, Ontario: Trinity Press, 1990.

Sangster, W. E., *The Craft of Sermon Illustration*, London: Epworth Press, 1946.

Schillebeeckx, Edward, *Christ the Sacrament of the Encounter with God*, New York: Sheed & Ward, 1963.

Schwöbel, Christoph, 'The Preacher's Art: Preaching Theologically', in *Theology through Preaching*, ed. Colin E. Gunton, Edinburgh: T. & T. Clark, 2001, pp. 1–20.

Searle, Alison, *'The Eyes of Your Heart': Literary and Theological Trajectories of Imagining Biblically*, Milton Keynes: Paternoster Press, 2008.

Smith, Christine M., *Weaving the Sermon: Preaching in a Feminist Perspective*, Louisville, KY: John Knox Press, 1989.

Soskice, Janet Martin, *Metaphor and Religious Language*, Oxford: Clarendon Press, 1985.

Stevenson, Geoffrey, 'Communication and Communion', in *Preaching with Humanity: A Practical Guide for Today's Church*, ed. Geoffrey Stevenson and Stephen Wright, London: Church House Publishing, 2008, pp. 94–107.

Tillich, Paul, *The Protestant Era*, Chicago: University of Chicago Press, 1957.

Tinsley, John, 'Communication, Or "Tell It Slant"', *Theology Today* 35:4 (1979), pp. 398–404.

Torrance, J. B., *Worship, Community, and the Triune God of Grace*, Downers Grove, IL: InterVarsity Press, 1996.

Tracy, David, *The Analogical Imagination: Christian Theology and Culture of Pluralism*, London: SCM Press, 1981.

Troeger, Thomas H., *Ten Strategies for Preaching in a Multi Media Culture*, Nashville, TN: Abingdon Press, 1996.

Trygve, David Johnson, *The Preacher as Artist: Metaphor, Identity, and the Vicarious Humanity of Christ*, PhD Thesis, University of St Andrews, 2010, http://research-repository.st-andrews.ac.uk/handle/10023/944.

Tubbs Tisdale, Leonora, *Preaching as Local Theology and Folk Art*, Minneapolis, MN: Fortress Press, 1997.

Van Hecke, P., 'Metaphor and Conceptual Blending', in *Metaphor in the Hebrew Bible*, ed. P. Van Hecke, Leuven: Peeters, 2005.

Ward, Richard F., 'Preaching as a Communicative Act: The Birth of a Performance', *Reformed Liturgy and Music* 30:2 (1996), www.religion-online.org/showarticle.asp?title=341.

Warnock, Mary, *Imagination*, London: Faber & Faber, 1976.

Warren, Mervyn A., *King Came Preaching*, Downers Grove, IL: InterVarsity Press, 2001.

Webb, Joseph, *Comedy and Preaching*, St Louis, MO: Chalice Press, 1998.

Webb, Stephen H., *The Divine Voice: Christian Proclamation and the Theology of Sound*, Grand Rapids, MI: Brazos Press, 2004.

Westerhoff, John, *Spiritual Life: The Foundation for Preaching and Teaching*, Louisville, KY: John Knox Press, 1994.

White, James F., *The Sacraments in Protestant Practice and Faith*, Nashville, TN: Abingdon Press, 1999.

Wiersbe, Warren, *Preaching and Teaching with Imagination: The Quest for Biblical Ministry*, Grand Rapids: MI: Baker, 1994.

Williams, Rowan, 'Sacraments of the New Society', in *Christ: The Sacramental Word*, ed. David Brown and Ann Loades, London: SPCK, 1996, pp. 89–101.

Williams, Rowan, 'Preface' to *The Gestures of God*, ed. Geoffrey Rowell and Christine Hall, London: Continuum, 2004, pp. xiii–xiv.

Willimon, William, *Conversations with Barth on Preaching*, Nashville, TN: Abingdon Press, 2006.

Wittgenstein, Ludwig, *Philosophical Investigations*, trans. G. E. M. Anscombe, London: Blackwell, 1968.

Index